God, Why Is This Happening?

The Cancer Patient's Book of Job

WHEN
CANCER
COMES

DAVID HAAG

T0307140

NORTHWESTERN PUBLISHING HOUSE

Milwaukee, Wisconsin

God, Why Is This Happening?

The Cancer Patient's Book of Job

DAVID HAAG

Cover: Photography by Devon Rose Liermann
Interior Layout: Mary Jaracz

Northwestern Publishing House
N16W23379 Stone Ridge Dr., Waukesha WI 53188-1108
www.nph.net
© 2024 by Northwestern Publishing House
Published 2024
Printed in the United States of America
ISBN 978-0-8100-2946-0
ISBN 978-0-8100-2947-7 (e-book)

24 25 26 27 28 29 30 31 32 33   10 9 8 7 6 5 4 3 2 1

In memory of Lisa,
God's greatest earthly gift to me.

FOREWORD

Share the story! Make it real and human. We are familiar with the principle. Reporters go to the site of breaking news and look for a witness to tell the story. They put a microphone in front of someone who has seen what happened. The words from someone who has been there and witnessed compel the story.

That principle stands behind this series of books entitled When Cancer Comes. We wanted to tell the story of cancer patients who struggled with their faith when the voice of Jesus seemed to evaporate in the heat of suffering. How did they find strength and comfort when cancer, like a hot coal, sizzled comfort away? We looked for writers who could tell their stories so that others could grow and find strength. We wanted their stories to be real and human.

Each author settled on a specific section of Scripture to help structure the story and message. One focused on Job, another on Paul, and another on Jeremiah. Each of these biblical characters had a special point to make while enduring pain and misery. Job wondered why God sent him so much suffering. Paul endured much but found a reason to boast even in his suffering. Jeremiah complained about his suffering and the suffering he saw around him.

These trials are not uncommon for cancer patients, so we asked the authors to tell their stories. They have been in the doctors' offices to hear the word *cancer*. They either have experienced the chemotherapy and weaknesses or have seen a loved one struggle with them. They matched their personal stories to these biblical characters and found ways to coax faith and courage to grow. In the soil of their dark days, God's promises nurtured the flower of faith.

Our prayer is that their stories help you water the flower of your faith using God's promises when your faith droops under each challenge.

John Braun, editor

Contents

Though he slay me,
yet will I hope in him.

Job 13:15

Introduction
"YOU'RE ASKING A QUESTION."

When I was a younger man, I hurt my knee. I had a torn ACL and some damage to my meniscus, but I didn't know all that immediately after the injury. I was referred to a very good orthopedic surgeon, Dr. Rubin. He was the official orthopedic doctor for the United States Olympic diving team. At my first visit with Dr. Rubin, he was explaining to me all of the things that might be wrong with my knee and some of the things he might be able to do to help me. "But I won't really know for sure until you get an MRI," he said. "After seeing the results of the MRI, I'll have a better idea of what to do next."

I started to ask a question. It was something like "If so-and-so is wrong with my knee and then you do such-and-such, will I be able to do this or that—like play basketball or go skiing?"

"You're asking a question," Dr. Rubin said, in a tone of voice that indicated I wasn't supposed to be asking questions.

"I know," I said. "Isn't a patient supposed to be able to ask questions of his doctor?"

"No," Dr. Rubin replied to my chagrin. "I told you that I won't really know your situation until after I see your MRI. Until then, you can't ask any questions," he said with a friendly smile.

It was not the kind of thing I expected to hear from my doctor: "You're not allowed to ask questions." But my doctor was right. It served no purpose to ask questions at that time. Eventually I had the MRI, and then Dr. Rubin answered all my questions and performed a successful surgery on my knee.

I had some questions, and the person I was asking, who I felt should have given me some answers, was not going to answer me. Christians have questions about many things in life. They want answers. In pain and misery, they have questions about how God is taking care of them. My experience paled in comparison to Job's pain thousands of years ago. My pain and discomfort were small next to Job's and also the pain of cancer patients now. But in a way they were similar. Ultimately, the book of Job in the Bible is about a man who had questions for God, questions that welled up from an intense pain most of us can't even begin to imagine. His questions were all the more anguished because of his emotional pain caused by people he thought were his friends and the fact that God did not answer his questions.

> The book of Job in the Bible is about a man who had questions for God, questions that welled up from an intense pain most of us can't even begin to imagine.

This book is for cancer sufferers and their families. It's not just for cancer patients. It's also for every believer who has ever suffered and had questions for God. In the Bible, God answers a lot of our questions, even our most important one: How do we get to be in the pain-free, cancer-free heaven with him? God provided that answer by sending his Son, Jesus, to live a perfect life in our place and die on the cross to pay for all our sins. Through faith in Jesus, we receive heaven. How to get to heaven is the most important question we could ever have, and in love for us, God clearly answers that question with Jesus.

Yet God does not answer all our questions in the Bible. In his wisdom and love, he decided that there are many answers we don't need to know, even though we may feel entitled to have them. That, I believe, is one of the messages of the book of Job.

Of course, this does not mean that God left Job or his people without comfort. The Bible gives us page after page of comfort. The book of Job teaches us to find God's comfort in what he has revealed to us and not to try to find comfort and answers where he has not revealed them to us. Just as parents do not answer all the questions their children ask, just as my doctor did not answer my questions that day in his office, so God does not answer all the burning questions that bubble up in our hearts when we are suffering pain. But just as parents still love their children, just as Dr. Rubin still had my best interests at heart, so God still loves us and has our best interests at heart. As you read this book, it is my prayer that you will be reminded of all the comfort your loving God has for you.

> Just as parents do not answer all the questions their children ask, . . . so God does not answer all the burning questions that bubble up in our hearts when we are suffering pain.

Chapter 1
A DAY IN THE LIFE OF LISA HAAG

March 13, 2014, dawned as just another day in the life of our family. At the age of 54, I was in the midst of my 19th year of teaching high school at Winnebago Lutheran Academy in Fond du Lac, Wisconsin. The big new challenge on my horizon was that after many years of coaching boys' soccer in the fall, I was getting ready that spring to start my first year of coaching girls' soccer as well. My wife, Lisa, also 54, went in that morning to her nanny job for a wonderful family. It was all pretty normal stuff in our blessed and happy life.

That day was a little more joyful than most because our youngest child and only daughter, Naomi, celebrated her 18th birthday. Our three older children, Andrew, Steven, and Jacob, were all out of the house and on their own. Our youngest was now 18, soon to graduate from high school and go off to college in the fall. Lisa and I would be empty nesters. Interesting but happy changes were on the horizon, we figured.

Oh, and also on that day, Lisa went in for her routine annual mammogram.

A day later, there was a message on the answering machine. The staff at the hospital called and said they noticed something on the mammogram. They wanted Lisa to come back in for a diagnostic mammogram and to be ready for an ultrasound as well.

We hoped that things would not be as bad as we feared. But then, it seemed, they always were.

1

Thus it began. For the next several weeks and months, we hoped that things would not be as bad as we feared. But then, it seemed, they always were.

After the answering machine message, Lisa told me that this had happened once before. On a previous occasion, the mammogram technician simply didn't get a clear picture and needed to redo the procedure. Maybe that's all this was. Maybe it's nothing to worry about.

But after a visual exam in the mirror, Lisa noticed a slight abnormality in the appearance of the surface of her right breast as compared to the left, and she had a sinking feeling of terror. She began to feel that this wasn't a technicality. Instead, she felt that this was going to be bad news. In her heart, she felt certain that she had cancer.

The next week Lisa went in for the diagnostic mammogram. It did indeed show an abnormal mass. So she immediately had an ultrasound to get a better picture of the situation. During the ultrasound, the radiologist asked several questions that led Lisa to fear the worst. The tears began to flow from her eyes.

We had questions: How bad could things be?

Lisa then needed a biopsy to see if the mass was cancerous or not. The cycle of hopefulness began again. Maybe the tumor was benign. That happened sometimes, right? Maybe it was benign and nothing further had to be done. That was often my attitude: Let's assume the best until we know otherwise. Our friends were encouraging and positive. In spite of all the positives, Lisa knew in her heart that she had cancer.

Lisa went in for the biopsy on March 25. That day turned out to be another day of birthday joy. When Lisa got home from the biopsy appointment, we received the news that our grandson Charlie was born that day to our son Steven and daughter-in-law Jackie. He is our third grandchild and first grandson. What joy!

Two days later, while taking care of the children at her nanny job, Lisa got the results of the biopsy. The breast health coordinator told her to get a notebook and take detailed notes of the pathology report she was about to give—not a good sign. The tumor was not benign. It was malignant and invasive. Lisa had cancer. She remembered, "When the diagnosis came, I realized how weak and terrified I was. It knocked me to my knees."

The cycle of hopes raised and hopes dashed continued. Sometimes you hear about how they caught it early. We thought maybe that's the case here. Maybe the doctors caught it early, and the tumor could be removed with minimal pain and invasiveness. We could hope, right?

> She remembered, "When the diagnosis came, I realized how weak and terrified I was. It knocked me to my knees."

Nope. The biopsy revealed that Lisa's breast cancer was a less common lobular type. It was not really a lump but a 3 to 5 millimeter wormlike mass that snaked around the tissue. The cancer specialists told us that lobular cancer is very difficult to detect on a regular mammogram until it is larger. The only way to remove the cancer was a complete mastectomy. Lisa pointed out that this was a nice way of saying "amputation." She could expect chemotherapy and radiation at some point after the operation.

Lisa underwent an MRI and another scan to see if the cancer had spread to her bones. These proved negative, for which we gave many thanks to God. It was one bit of good news in a mostly unending series of bad news in the early days of Lisa's cancer experience.

The surgery was scheduled as soon as possible. At this point, the surgeon thought the cancer was at stage 2. Stage 4 is the most advanced. When you are diagnosed with stage 4 cancer, you usually do not have too many more months to live. So all things considered at that point, stage 2 didn't sound too life-threatening. But things would change.

On April 7, Lisa went in for her operation. We knew the surgeon was going to remove Lisa's right breast and, hopefully, all of the cancer from her body. But during the operation, the doctor checked the sentinel lymph node in the area of Lisa's armpit and discovered it was cancerous. She checked another lymph node. It also was cancerous. In total, she removed 19 lymph nodes, all of which subsequently proved to be cancerous. This meant that Lisa's cancer was reclassified as stage 3. In the pit of our stomachs, our fears grew. We wondered if something else was going to turn up and show her cancer was stage 4. We dreaded to find out.

Because of the removal of the lymph nodes and the mastectomy surgery, Lisa would have to deal with pain and complications in her right arm for the rest of her life. She would experience nerve pain, phantom pain, and possible swelling among other things. This condition is known as lymphedema. Life was going from bad to worse.

> Christians have questions, but God does not always answer them.

What next?

In the introduction, I shared how sometimes Christians have questions, but God does not always answer them. Throughout 2014, as Lisa and I lived through her cancer diagnosis, operation, and subsequent treatment, we usually asked what was going to happen next. How could this get any worse? From an earthly point of view, it often did.

But we also knew that on every step of the way, our gracious God would be with us and our Savior, Jesus, who loved us so much that he gave his life for us, would help us, give us strength, and calm our fears. If God deemed it best to give us answers to our questions, he would. If not, we knew we could still put our hope and trust in him.

Job had different questions.

Chapter 2
ANOTHER DAY IN THE LIFE

This day was not a day in March 2014. It was a specific date on the ancient calender probably three to four thousand years ago. It wasn't Fond du Lac, Wisconsin. It was the land of Uz, somewhere in the Middle East. It wasn't a day in the life of Lisa and David Haag. It was a day in the life of Job, and it probably started like most days in his life.

The day came as one more in a happy and blessed life. Job was a rich man. In his days, wealth was not measured in dollars, bank accounts, 401(k) funds, big houses, and late model cars. Wealth was measured in flocks and herds: sheep, cattle, oxen, donkeys, and camels. They provided food and clothing and were the cars, trucks, heavy machinery, and luxury vehicles of the day. They were the currency of the day because they could be sold or bartered for other needs, luxuries, or comforts. A person's financial security was also measured in children and servants. In the absence of today's hospitals and nursing homes, children and servants would take care of someone as he or she aged. They were the investment portfolio and retirement plan.

All this Job had in abundance. Just as the wealth of some in today's world is mind-boggling, so it was with Job. By the standards of his day, the numbers were stratospheric. Job 1:2,3 tells us he possessed seven thousand sheep, three thousand camels, five hundred yokes of oxen, five hundred donkeys, and "a large number of servants." Best of all, he boasted of seven sons and three daughters. His children seemed to have happy, carefree lives as well. They would regularly get together for eating, drinking, and feasting. Job had it all—wealth, a loving family, good health.

And then one day . . .

> The sick feeling of terror grew in the pit of his stomach. Still more serious news, but he could recover from this blow over time.
>
> It couldn't get worse, could it?

Job was at home, probably tending to his usual affairs. Perhaps he was looking after his vast holdings. He knew that his children were at his oldest son's home. They were again "feasting and drinking wine" (Job 1:13). It must have been a festive day, perhaps a birthday or the birth of a grandchild. Job was no doubt thinking about them.

And then . . .

Seemingly out of nowhere, a servant breathlessly rode up to Job and brought him devastating news: "The oxen were plowing and the donkeys were grazing nearby, and the Sabeans attacked and made off with them. They put the servants to the sword, and I am the only one who has escaped to tell you!" (Job 1:14,15).

What a punch to the gut! If I were Job at this point, I'm sure my heart would have started racing. The servants and a part of his wealth were gone.

Things couldn't get worse, could they?

Another servant came running up: "The fire of God [quite possibly lightning] fell from the heavens and burned up the sheep and the servants, and I am the only one who has escaped to tell you!" (Job 1:16).

More racing of the heart. The sick feeling of terror grew in the pit of his stomach. Still more serious news, but he could recover from this blow over time.

It couldn't get worse, could it?

Then came a third servant: "The Chaldeans formed three raiding parties and swept down on your camels and made off with them. They put the servants to the sword, and I am the only one who has escaped to tell you!" (Job 1:17).

How could this be? Job lost everything. He was no longer a rich man. Can you try to feel what he was feeling? Can you imagine the feeling of looking at the smoking hulk of your burned-down house, the overwhelming gloom of knowing all your possessions were gone? Your bank account wiped out. Your home, your cars . . . everything was up in smoke. Gone forever. What a frightened, sickening feeling I would have in the pit of my stomach. I might faint or sit down and let the silent tears flow down my cheeks.

This couldn't get any worse, could it?

But then it did. The cruelest blow of all came with the next servant's message. He said that Job's children "were . . . at the oldest brother's house, when suddenly a mighty wind swept in from the desert and struck the four corners of the house. It collapsed on them and they are dead, and I am the only one who has escaped to tell you!" (Job 1:18,19).

This was the worst news. If my car and credit cards were stolen or my house burned down, it would be unspeakably devastating. But I would quickly give those away rather than suffer the death of even one child, much less all my children. Maybe some of you have gotten that dreadful phone call, "Your child was involved in a car accident . . ." I can't imagine a more devastating moment.

> Job had reached the bottom of the pit of despair.

Job had reached the bottom of the pit of despair. He "got up and tore his robe and shaved his head" (Job 1:20). These were signs of deepest sorrow and anguish. Who could blame him?

If you were Job, would you have questions? "What is going on? How could all this happen to me? Where is God? Isn't he a loving God? I have lived an upright life, so how could God let this happen? What is his plan in all this?"

> At this point in Job's life, . . . he didn't direct bitter questions at God. He simply expressed his trust in God and acceptance of whatever would come from God's hand.

I would have questions. At this point the Bible does not say that Job asked any pained questions of God. The first verse of the book of Job says that he "was blameless and upright; he feared God and shunned evil." At this point in Job's life, he showed that this was true. Even though his heart was broken and all his wealth was gone, he didn't wave his fist in anger at God. He didn't direct bitter questions at God. He simply expressed his trust in God and acceptance of whatever would come from God's hand. Job's words are truly remarkable: "Naked I came from my mother's womb, and naked I will depart. The LORD gave and the LORD has taken away; may the name of the LORD be praised" (Job 1:21).

Of course, it couldn't get worse. Right?

Chapter 3
"THIS IS REALLY STARTING TO SUCK"

On April 7, 2014, Lisa underwent her mastectomy. We learned that her cancer had spread to the lymph nodes. For the next several weeks, she recovered at home. She experienced a lot of pain and discomfort from the drainage tubes the surgeon had inserted into her right side. Her right side, as you could well imagine, was bruised and heavily taped and bandaged. Burning infection set in. Tears often flowed down her cheeks. When it came time to take the tape and bandages off, that was an ordeal. I'm sure that all of this is familiar to those who have gone through invasive surgery.

More appointments followed. On April 24, Lisa had a CT scan of her lungs and abdomen to see if the cancer had spread to those areas. The fact it had spread to 19 of her lymph nodes raised the fear that it had spread elsewhere. At this point, to hear that her cancer had metastasized to her lungs or beyond would have felt like a death sentence.

But there was good news—sort of—and also bad news—sort of. The scan revealed that there were no definite carcinomas anywhere, the key word being *definite*. Yet there were two or three very small nodules on Lisa's lungs. The doctor said they were too small to characterize or explore with a biopsy. Lisa had suffered a lot from bronchitis in her younger years, so the nodules could just be scars from those previous illnesses—*or* they could be cancerous.

What now? Again, that was the question. We would have to wait until after Lisa started the dreaded chemotherapy. After a few months of chemo, she would undergo another scan. If the spots on her lungs were smaller, that would actually be bad news. It would mean that the spots were cancerous and the chemo was shrinking them. The ideal outcome would be that they stayed the same size. If the chemo didn't affect them, that would indicate they were noncancerous.

> After getting this latest piece of news, our daughter, Naomi, said, "This is really starting to suck."

For the moment, we did not know. There was no answer, just questions. The good and bad news gave us an uncertain hope—no definite carcinomas—but also a queasy fear—those spots could be cancerous.

After getting this latest piece of news, our daughter, Naomi, said, "This is really starting to suck."

Our sentiments exactly.

Not heroes, just sufferers

Kairol Rosenthal was 27 years old and living her interesting single life in San Francisco when she was diagnosed with stage 2 thyroid cancer. After going through treatment, she went around the country interviewing other young adult cancer patients. The result is her fascinating book *Everything Changes*. One consistent theme for these 20- and 30-somethings is that they don't see themselves as heroic survivors full of pluck and wisdom. That's the popular Hallmark Channel image of cancer sufferers. These young adults are going through pain, and they often feel desperate, depressed, and angry.

As we continued to get one discouraging piece of news after another in Lisa's cancer journey, we could relate. If you are going through or have gone through cancer treatment, you know. If you are a loved one of a cancer patient, you also can relate. There is no sugarcoating it: Cancer stinks. It involves pain, suffering, and depression. Most people I know who have gone through cancer echo the thoughts of Kairol Rosenthal. Cancer is not ennobling. It does not convey some mystical insight into life, making cancer patients into gurus. Our daughter was right. After a while, cancer really starts to suck.

So our question, as usual, was "What's next, Lord?" There would be a lot more pain, a lot more fear. A lot of waiting and a lot of unknowns. But God was also with us every step of the way, helping Lisa through the pain, calming our fears. He was also helping me as I watched, helpless in my own secondary pain. Along with Job, we could say, "The Lord gave [times of health and happiness] and the Lord has taken away [Lisa's health and our life together]; may the name of the Lord be praised." We had a lot of unanswered questions, but we also knew that God would take care of us. It remained to be seen how he would do that, but we knew we were in his hands.

> Our question, as usual, was "What's next, Lord?"

Chapter 4
IT GETS WORSE FOR JOB

Once numbered among the richest, Job and his wife were now destitute. Once a life enriched with a happy family, his heart broke every day as he grieved for his beloved children. They were gone from his life. His life couldn't get any worse.

And then it did.

One day, painful sores began to appear on Job's body. Not just one or two on his arms where he could easily attend to them. No, they covered his entire body. They were even on the bottoms of his feet and the top of his head.

> Job shared his misery, "Nights of misery have been assigned to me."

We have all had a pesky insect bite that makes us want to scratch it for some temporary relief, but it still persists for a few days and doesn't go away. It can be maddening. Job's sores were infinitely worse, so bad that he scraped himself with broken pottery to try to get some relief. Not very sanitary. It would seem that the sharp edges of the broken pottery would cause a lot of pain. Why would you want to voluntarily scrape yourself with that? But that's how intense Job's misery was—scraping his raw skin with pottery was preferable to the agony he was enduring.

And then it got worse.

Job shared his misery, "Nights of misery have been assigned to me. When I lie down I think, 'How long before I get up?' The night drags on, and I toss and turn until dawn. My body is clothed with worms and scabs, my skin is broken and festering" (Job 7:3-5). He even refused to eat because it made him ill (Job 6:6,7). The friends who came to visit him could hardly recognize him, and they wept when they saw him. Job's appearance was mangled beyond previous recognition. Can you even begin to imagine how disgusting Job must have felt? His pain and suffering were severe: "The churning inside me never stops. My skin grows black and peels; my body burns with fever" (Job 30:27,30). What a nightmare!

Cancer sufferers, can you relate to Job's misery?

Job's pain was so hideous that his wife couldn't bear to see it anymore. She asked him, "Are you still maintaining your integrity? Curse God and die!" (Job 2:9). Apparently her thinking was "Nothing, even hell, could be worse than what you are suffering, Job. If you curse the God who has allowed this into your life, surely he can't punish you any more than what you are now suffering." If she had believed in God as a gracious and loving God, her faith was challenged and on life support.

> If I was Job, I would have been filled with questions.

If I was Job, I would have been filled with questions: "Why is this happening to me? Haven't I suffered enough, Lord? Are you punishing me, Lord? What have I done? What is going on?"

Once rich and now penniless, once a happy family man and now mourning ten children and married to a wife harping on him to curse God, Job and his faith were taking a beating. Once healthy and strong and now a hideous, scab-encrusted shell racked with fever, it seems Job would have had every right to follow his wife's advice. Once a respected leader of his community and now an object of horror and pity, no one could blame Job for giving up on God.

Instead, we have one of the most amazing confessions of faith in the entire Bible. Job's response to his wife was simply to endure and remain faithful to the Lord. He told her, "Shall we accept good from God, and not trouble?" The author of the book of Job adds, "In all this, Job did not sin in what he said" (Job 2:10). Job's trust in God is almost beyond comprehension.

At this point, so far, so good for Job. He lost everything, but his faith was steadfast. He displayed his legendary patience. So far, so good, at least for his faith, right?

Things were about to get interesting.

Chapter 5
YOUR STORY

I have shared the beginning of Lisa's cancer experience. I have also detailed the beginning of Job's story to you. What is your story?

Because if you have experience with cancer or a loved one who has suffered through cancer, you also have a story. You are not alone. According to the National Cancer Institute, 38.5 percent of people in the US will have some kind of cancer at some point in their lives. That's about four out of ten people. If you yourself don't get cancer in your life, the chances are pretty good that your spouse, parent, or child will.

My mom died of cancer. My grandfather died of cancer 15 years before I was born. I can't begin to count all the relatives, friends, fellow church members, and others close to me who have had cancer. Sooner or later, it seems to touch everyone in some way.

> Everyone's cancer story is unique. Cancer does not come in one form but many forms, and it attacks all different parts of the body.

Everyone's cancer story is unique. Cancer does not come in one form but many forms, and it attacks all different parts of the body. Each case is different in its severity. On one end of the spectrum, some people have a minimally severe cancer. These people suffer no great pain or inconvenience from cancer. They don't require painful treatment or need powerful drugs, chemo, or radiation. The doctors just keep an eye on it. Life goes on pretty much the same as before, although with the heavy and threatening cloud of cancer always hovering overhead. Maybe that's the story of you or your loved one.

On the other end of the spectrum, some people have a cancer that attacks and overruns their body quickly. These people suffer through painful treatments that do no good, and cancer robs them of their life with breathtaking speed. As I was writing this book, I remembered a wonderful Christian man in one of our Lutheran churches. He was seemingly a picture of health, but then he discovered that he had advanced-stage cancer. It spread so quickly that he died within two months. Such cases are not rare. Maybe that's the story of you or your loved one.

You are probably somewhere in between those extremes.

> I would like to tell you the story of my friends Mike and his wife, Jennifer.

I would like to tell you the story of my friends Mike and his wife, Jennifer. I think that their experience is similar to Job's experience and perhaps yours as well.

Mike was a member of our church in Fond du Lac. In March 2014, the same month Lisa learned that she had cancer, so did Mike. He was 58 years old. He had quit smoking shortly before, and he had had a lung scan a few months prior that indicated his lungs were cancer-free. He heard about a new test for former smokers to check for signs of lung cancer more accurately. He just wanted to make extra sure.

This new scan indicated once again that there was no cancer in Mike's lungs. But it unexpectedly revealed a cancerous tumor in his kidney. Not only that, but the cancer had also spread throughout his bones. Suddenly, he discovered his situation was terminal.

Mike and Jennifer have one son, Christopher, who was a sophomore in high school that year. The couple knew that Mike would die from this cancer, but their hope looked for a way to help their son. Could they buy Mike enough time that he might get to see Christopher through his high school years and help guide him to college? Could they alleviate Mike's suffering so that this could happen?

So the ordeal began. Mike was put on a cancer drug that hopefully would help. He went back in after a month or so. The cancer drug was doing no good at all. Mike's cancer continued to spread. His suffering increased. He was given a second cancer drug, which also proved to be ineffective. His pain got worse. His condition continued to deteriorate.

Mike and Jennifer went to Mayo Clinic. Mike was put into a trial program along with many other advanced-stage cancer patients. He underwent several torturous tests to see if anything could be done for him. At the end of the tests, half of the participants would be given a trial drug that looked very promising. Hope entered the hearts of the couple. If Mike could get this drug, his suffering would be alleviated, at least for a while, and his life would be extended. The other half of the participants would receive an existing drug that wasn't as promising. A random draw determined who got which drug.

As a result of the draw, Mike was assigned the traditional drug, not the trial one. It also did not help. Jennifer remembered feeling, "Why can't we ever get a break? Why is it always one piece of bad news after another? Why does my husband have to suffer like this?" She had a lot of questions, just as Job eventually did.

The more promising, experimental drug was not approved by the FDA, and so it was not covered by insurance. Mike's doctor felt very strongly that the experimental drug would help, but the cost of paying for this drug without insurance was prohibitive. Mike was very frustrated by the results of the random draw and the insurance company's inability to pay for the trial drug. So Jennifer petitioned the insurance company to reconsider. Eventually, it did. But after going through all this red tape, it was now

September, and it was too late. Around the same time that Lisa was finishing up her chemotherapy in October 2014, Mike died, seven months after learning that he had cancer.

Like us—like Job—Jennifer trusts in God and knows that Jesus is her Savior. She is not a bitter and angry person. She is a happy person, and a big part of her happiness is knowing that her beloved Mike is in heaven with his Savior. But during Mike's cancer experience, she had questions and still does. During those months of 2014, they would often feel hope evaporate when they went to the doctor. Both asked, "Why does it always have to be bad news? This drug isn't working. You can't get this drug that might help. You can, but now it's too late. Why?"

> Jennifer's questions for God remain. Why did her husband have to suffer so much? Why do other children get to have their father, but Christopher was robbed of his?

Jennifer's questions for God remain. Why did her husband have to suffer so much? Why do other children get to have their father, but Christopher was robbed of his? It doesn't seem completely fair or loving. It doesn't seem like the kind of thing a loving God would do. Sometimes God seems arbitrary and indecipherable.

Maybe you have similar questions.

Back to Job. By the end of Job chapter 2, he had not asked any bitter questions of God. But soon he would.

Chapter 6
WITH FRIENDS LIKE THESE

Job's life turned into one bad report after another. It all started one fine day when the first bombshell struck. His possessions were suddenly gone. Then a messenger told him that his children were also gone. The bad news continued. Sores over his entire body plagued him each day. His body was wracked with pain, and then his wife was repulsed by him. He was once an honored man in his community. Now he was nothing more than an object of scorn and pity. It couldn't get worse, right?

> Now he was nothing more than an object of scorn and pity. It couldn't get worse, right?

Well, it did. Meet Job's *friends*: Eliphaz, Bildad, and Zophar.

These three friends came to sympathize with Job and comfort him. From a distance, they could hardly recognize him, so they wept, tore their robes to indicate the depth of their distress, and sprinkled dust on their heads. It was a grievous shock. They sat with him for seven days without speaking "because they saw how great his suffering was" (Job 2:13). Job finally spoke. His legendary patience was no more. In the presence of his friends, he lamented his horrendous pain and repeatedly wished that he had never been born. Job expressed his faith several times throughout the conversation, but he was beginning to crack under the crushing burden of his pain. Who could blame him?

The conversation of Job with his friends is the heart and core of the book of Job. Let's explore it.

But first, some wisdom from Mom

I can remember one day when I was kid, I think I was 11 or 12 years old, and I was complaining to my mom about some other kids in my school who were getting away with cheating on their homework. I remember my mom's motherly wisdom. She said, "Well, those kids will eventually suffer the consequences of their cheating. Maybe they're not getting caught right now, but later they will. When it comes time for the tests, they will fail, because they didn't do their homework honestly so they won't know the material." She continued, "Then their laziness and cheating will be exposed and come back to haunt them. If this becomes their habit, they will have trouble later holding a job because they will be lazy and employers will hold them responsible for that." My mom was teaching me that in this life, people generally suffer the consequences of their actions. They reap what they sow. She wanted to encourage me not to worry about those kids who seemed to be getting away with their cheating. Sooner or later, they would get what they had coming to them. She wanted me to keep doing what was right.

I remember being comforted by my mom's words. And even now, so many years later, I think most of us would agree that what my mom said is true. Generally, people who work hard and are honest and good to their neighbors have good reputations and are treated well. Generally, people who cheat and are crooked and dishonest are exposed and punished. Of course, there are exceptions, but the general rule works for most people.

And that's how it usually works in the movies. At the end of *The Shawshank Redemption*, the warden is exposed as the evil hypocrite that he is, the sadistic guards are arrested and go to jail, and Tim Robbins and Morgan Freeman enjoy the sunshine on the beach in Mexico. At the end of *A Few Good Men*, the haughty Jack Nicholson is brought to justice, and the virtuous Tom Cruise gloats.

I'm sure you can remember some movies you have watched in which the good guy finally succeeds. You end up with a good feeling, encouraged to do what is right. In this life people get what they deserve: Good people get good things, and bad people get bad things. For the most part, that was the message of Job's friends. Hmmm. But is that really true? More important, is that a comforting message to a suffering person? To a man who was suffering horribly, this was not very comforting. Job clearly found no comfort in the conversation with his friends.

> Good people get good things, and bad people get bad things. . . . Hmmm. But is that really true?

One man's attempt to make sense of the conversation between Job and his friends

One of the reasons I was excited to write this book was that the book of Job has always fascinated me, but it has also puzzled me. The first two chapters are straightforward prose telling the tragedy that befell Job. It is pretty easy to retell that story in chronological order.

> Job expressed so many good thoughts about God's majesty and power, but he also expressed some contradictory thoughts.

The next 35 chapters of Job are not always so easy to follow and summarize. One reason is that Job and his friends lived thousands of years ago in a culture much different from ours. This was not a group of friends sitting around a coffee shop speaking contemporary English. Another reason is that the conversation is recorded in poetic form, so it is not as easy for modern readers to follow along as it would be if it were just straightforward dialogue.

But I think the main reason it's hard to summarize is that Job expressed so many good thoughts about God's majesty and power, but he also expressed some contradictory thoughts. He claimed to be one of the good guys and wanted to make his case before God. Again and again he asked, "Why are you doing this to me, Lord? I'm one of the good guys." The more I read this conversation, the more I am puzzled by it and find it hard to summarize.

But here goes . . .

The friends were pretty consistent in their message. They said, "Here's the deal, Job. God punishes the wicked—the proud, the powerful, those who don't submit to him. He rewards good and humble people." Their message to Job was like my mom's message to me so many years ago.

This leads to a conclusion that is sometimes only implied and other times directly expressed. Since God punishes the wicked and rewards the good, Job obviously was suffering horribly because he committed some kind of grievous sin. Therefore, the only answer the friends could find was that Job needed to repent and turn to God. Then God would bless him and everything would be great again.

In Job's responses, he was all over the place. At one point, he agreed with his friends. He said, "Indeed, I know that this is true" (Job 9:2); that is, that God punished the wicked but rewarded the good. But that's exactly why he was perplexed. He was innocent, so why was God punishing him? It didn't make any sense to him. Sometimes Job admitted he was a sinner. Most often, he protested his innocence.

Usually, Job disagreed with his friends and said it was obvious that God allows and even sends calamity to good people and allows evil people to prosper. Often Job seemed to complain against God: that God was being too harsh with him. Occasionally he expressed his faith in God as a loving God. Sometimes he expressed awe and admiration for God, for his almighty power and just way of dealing with humans. Sometimes he expressed the desire to confront God and have God explain himself. At other times he said he knew that such an idea was folly: God didn't have to answer him and wasn't going to do so anyway. Sometimes he expressed the desire for an advocate, like a lawyer, to go between him and God. Sometimes he expressed his confidence that he had such an advocate.

Sometimes Job expressed agony that God was too distant and unapproachable, apparently unconcerned about Job. Other times, he expressed the opposite: God was too concerned about Job, too close to him, watching him like a hawk, stalking him, ready to punish him for the slightest misstep. Over and over again, he described his pain and anguish. He seemed to be asking his friends, "Do you really understand what I'm going through?"

Why was Job all over the place? Well, put yourself in his shoes. You are suffering unimaginable pain, and now your friends are yelling at you that it is your fault. You are perplexed and confused by what is happening. After going through everything Job had gone through, his thoughts and emotions were even more topsy-turvy. To me, it is no wonder that his line of thinking is not always so easy to follow.

> Are you like Job? Topsy-turvy emotions and thoughts race within and sometimes spill out in challenges to God about what he is doing to you and to your family.

Your cancer or the cancer of the one you love has stirred your questions. Are you like Job? Topsy-turvy emotions and thoughts race within and sometimes spill out in challenges to God about what he is doing to you and to your family. You wonder what you did to deserve this trouble. You know there was nothing. You too claim innocence because you did nothing to deserve such treatment, perhaps even calling it punishment. Your questions and thoughts churn with no answers.

One thing is obvious as the conversation goes around and around in these chapters: Job was not comforted by his friends. He got angrier and angrier at them. They in turn got more and more frustrated with him. They talked past one another. They insulted one another. The friends originally showed up at Job's door to comfort him, but they didn't. They consistently thought they were being helpful, but they weren't.

> This led Job to have questions. "Why is this happening to me? Why doesn't anyone understand me? Does even God understand?"

This led Job to have questions. "Why is this happening to me? Why doesn't anyone understand me? Does even God understand? This doesn't make any sense, according to the way God is supposed to deal with people. I want God to explain himself to me." Job cried out, "Let the Almighty answer me" (Job 31:35).

Will God answer Job's questions? If so, what will the answers be?

Chapter 7
THE YEAR 2014 COMES TO
AN END FOR LISA

Remember that we learned of Lisa's cancer in March 2014. In April, Lisa had surgery to remove her right breast, and the doctor also removed 19 cancerous lymph nodes. After weeks of painful recovery from the surgery, the doctors discovered spots on her lungs. We were hopeful the spots were only scars from her earlier bronchitis. We had to wait for months to see if they were also cancerous. If they were, that would mean the cancer had begun to spread to the rest of her body, and her long-term prognosis would have been quite gloomy. Lisa would have to wait out the stomach-churning uncertainty, much like Job waited for an answer from God.

So what's next? On May 2, we had our first meeting with the oncologist. After considering Lisa's case, he recommended the dreaded chemotherapy for Lisa. The first of four rounds was on May 22. It was Adriamycin and Cytoxan, a pretty powerful combination of chemo drugs, administered every two weeks. The combination is nicknamed "the Red Devil" in cancer circles. After every chemotherapy treatment, Lisa went in the next day to get a shot of Neulasta. That caused her intense bone and muscle pain. Then starting in mid-July, Lisa received Taxol, another chemo drug, every week for 12 weeks, ending on October 3. After that, she had a respite of a month, after which she started radiation—every day, Monday through Friday, for six weeks, ending on December 18.

Anticipating the chemo after surgery, Lisa thought, "I can do surgery and radiation. But I'm not strong enough for chemo." Then when the doctor talked about four rounds of the Red Devil, Lisa began to think, "Okay. . . . I can get through four rounds of that, but no more." But there was more. When Lisa heard the devastating news that she would have 12 more weekly rounds of chemo, she was terrified. She felt, "I am not strong enough for that. God will have to get me through this because I can't do it on my own."

> She felt, "I am not strong enough for that. God will have to get me through this because I can't do it on my own."

After the first four rounds of chemo, Lisa then had to stare down 12 more weeks of Taxol. For her that was overwhelming. Panic occasionally set in. The prospect of 12 more rounds was emotionally and physically daunting.

If you or a loved one has had cancer, you know that there are countless kinds of cancers and countless ways of treating them in our modern world. Lisa's chemo ordeal was unique to her, but her side effects were familiar to most cancer patients. She lost her lovely hair. She dealt with nausea and various other stomach and intestinal ailments. She had unexpected and unexplained pain in various parts of her body. She had dealt with migraines for years, but chemo caused even more headaches. She experienced fevers and infections. She had sores in her mouth. We dealt with constant fears about infection and had to be hypervigilant about exposure to anything that would set her back.

I never knew before that many cancer patients who receive chemo intravenously, as Lisa did, need to have a port surgically inserted. The chemo treatment is injected into the body through that port. It alleviates the need for endless needle poking into someone's arm or some other part of the body. The port is inserted before the first chemo treatment and isn't removed until all the treatments are over. Lisa's port was inserted a little below her collarbone. It was painful when inserted and both painful and inconvenient throughout the four and a half months of chemo. It was removed with one more surgery. Even after the port's removal in October, Lisa stayed sore for a long time. She has a bright red, noticeable scar there that she will always have.

In the midst of the months of chemo, Lisa went in for a scan on July 24 to look at those worrisome spots on her lungs. Good news! They had not changed, indicating they were not cancerous. We prayed many prayers of thanks that day.

After Lisa's last radiation treatment on December 18, we celebrated Christmas and New Year's with a little more joy, giving thanks to our gracious Lord for guiding her through the months of treatment. Back when the chemo started, Lisa knew she couldn't get through it without our Lord Jesus, and he gave her the strength to endure. We also gave thanks, and still are thankful, for all the wonderful medical people at the hospital and cancer center who took care of her. We had a lot of questions along the way, and the Lord answered most of them. We especially gave thanks, and still give thanks, for our many Christian friends who helped us through those dark days.

> We especially gave thanks, and still give thanks, for our many Christian friends who helped us through those dark days.

Finishing chemo and radiation has not meant the end of Lisa's cancer road. She still needs to take the oral cancer drug Exemestane every day for ten years to help lower the chance of recurrence. She has suffered health complications as the result of the cancer and chemotherapy. Every time she experiences a new and unexplained pain somewhere, she has to deal with the fear that the cancer has come back. She must now avoid many foods she used to enjoy because they can act as fertilizer to her type of cancer. As of this writing, Lisa has been cancer-free since her treatment. It is something for which we give thanks to God every day.

> The doctors tell us that she has a 30 percent chance of recurrence.

Even after all of Lisa's treatment and all the precautions she takes, the doctors tell us that she has a 30 percent chance of recurrence. Lisa still has scars from the surgery and treatment that remind her every day of the cancer cloud hanging over her. Will her cancer come back? How many more years of cancer-free living will Lisa have? Why did she get cancer in the first place? These are questions that God doesn't answer for us.

How about for Job? How did his story end? What were the answers to his questions?

Chapter 8
GOD ANSWERS

Job lost everything. Why? His children died. Why? He was suffering unrelenting and debilitating pain. Why? His friends had the answer. They thought that God was obviously punishing Job for some wickedness he had kept secret. Their solution was simple: Confess your secret wickedness, Job, and God will bless you and everything will be great again.

Job questioned that party line. He knew it wasn't true. He was not guilty of some terrible sin. So what was really going on? After his intense sufferings, after enduring the accusations of his friends, Job wanted answers: "Oh, that I had someone to hear me! . . . Let the Almighty answer me" (Job 31:35).

Finally, at the end of the book, Job got his wish. God spoke for four chapters (Job 38–41). But it was a little shocking and unsatisfying. He did not say one word about Job's suffering. He did not address Job's questions. He did not tell Job why he was suffering.

> God . . . did not address Job's questions. He did not tell Job why he was suffering.

Huh? How can this be? Isn't that exactly what Job had been waiting for throughout the conversation with his friends? He wanted answers to his questions. Isn't that the whole point of the book? As we read it, we expect that God is going to explain why Job and we Christians suffer.

God apparently had other thoughts. He began by saying, "Who is this that obscures my plans with words without knowledge? Brace yourself like a man; I will question you, and you shall answer me" (Job 38:2,3). Job had questions for God but no answers. Instead of answers to Job's questions, God said, "I have questions for you, Job."

God asked, "Where were you when I laid the earth's foundation?" (Job 38:4). The answer was obvious: Job was nowhere to be found when God created the universe. The point was obvious: Job was merely a creature of the almighty Creator of the universe. Job did not have the right to question God's ways and his dealings with humans.

God's questions continued like this for four chapters. God asked Job if he understood why the seas and oceans have the boundaries that they have. He asked Job if he understood where light, darkness, wind, and rain come from. Did Job control the movement of the stars? Did Job understand all the ways of the animals and what they do in secret far away from human eyes? By comparison with God's almighty, awesome power and the majesty and beauty of his creation, Job was insignificant. So are we all.

Then God spoke from a storm and described two fearsome creatures, translated as "Behemoth" and "Leviathan" in the NIV Bible. The descriptions are poetic so we do not know for sure what animals are being described—maybe a hippopotamus, an elephant, a crocodile, or even some unknown and now extinct animal. It's a little mysterious what these creatures were, but the point was clear. God was saying to Job, "I created these fearsome creatures. I control them. Job, can you do what I do? Can you even begin to understand me?" Obviously, the answer is no.

God was not going to answer Job's questions. God would remain hidden to Job at least on this point. The answer to Job's main question, "Why is this happening to me?" remained a mystery of the almighty God. Job would have to be satisfied with that.

And he was. Job finally said to God, "I know that you can do all things; no purpose of yours can be thwarted. Surely I spoke of things I did not understand, things too wonderful for me to know. My ears had heard of you but now my eyes have seen you. Therefore I despise myself and repent in dust and ashes" (Job 42:2,3,5,6). Job did not abandon his understanding of God's power, majesty, and control of all things. Job was troubled by the reason God did what he did. But ultimately Job was content with the knowledge that God is a God who does not reveal the answers to all our questions, just as my orthopedic doctor did not answer my questions. Just as oncologists can't always answer their patients' questions.

> Job was content with the knowledge that God is a God who does not reveal the answers to all our questions.

The book ends with God rebuking the three friends and commending Job. "He said to Eliphaz the Temanite, 'I am angry with you and your two friends, because you have not spoken the truth about me, as my servant Job has'" (Job 42:7). In the last verses of the book, God blessed Job with greater blessings than he had at the beginning.

I think all this leaves us unsatisfied and perhaps even filled with more questions. We are told to search the Scriptures for answers, but here there are none. God remains a mystery about some things. Is there anything he tells us that helps us as we face life's trials, especially cancer's intrusion into our lives and the lives of our loved ones? There must be. So many have turned to the Scriptures for comfort, strength, and answers. We know what God does not tell us, but let's look at what he does tell us.

> God remains a mystery about some things.

Chapter 9
WHAT TO MAKE OF
THIS MYSTERIOUS BOOK

Job wanted an answer to his question, "Why is God allowing pain and misery in my life?" His friends offered no answer except to accuse Job of some dark and secret sin as the reason for God punishing him. God himself provided no answer; he asserted that he does not give answers to all our questions. The book of Job leaves us unsatisfied with no answer to why we suffer.

Why is this book in the Bible then? Is there another way of looking at the whys of life that can be helpful and comforting? Is there anything we can learn from the Bible that will make sense? Or is the Bible like all the other self-help books but only worse because it gives no answers? I don't want this book to be too theological or "Bible classy." But in order to explain

> I want to explore another way of looking at God and our suffering.

and apply the mysterious book of Job to the lives of people in general and the lives of cancer patients in specific, I want to explore another way of looking at God and our suffering. Please bear with me.

The hidden God

I teach high school Spanish. When students ask me, "What does *amable* mean in English?" I can answer. If they ask, "What is the infinitive of this verb?" or "How do you say *grandfather* in

Spanish?" I can answer their questions. Easy, right? At least for a Spanish teacher.

I also teach high school religion. My students have a lot of questions about that too. They ask questions, just as Christians have asked their pastors for generations. Some of those questions are troubling to them: "Why doesn't God just destroy all the evil and bloodshed in this world? Why did God allow my mom or dad to die? If God wants all people to be saved, then why doesn't he just save all people?" My answer is often "I don't know." I answer that way because God has not revealed the answers to many of those questions in the Bible. Sometimes my students are satisfied with that answer. Sometimes they even respect that answer, because they have gotten answers in the past that were confusing to them. At other times they'd rather hear that there is no answer than a bewildering answer. But perhaps they have come to realize that not all questions have a clear answer.

> Not all questions have a clear answer.

I know that some of my students just get frustrated and angry with me for saying, "I don't know." They want answers and I am a pastor. Pastors are supposed to be able to answer all their questions about God, right? A lot of times they are like Martin Sixsmith.

"They'll probably say he moves in mysterious ways."

Who is Martin Sixsmith?

One of the movies nominated for the Academy Awards in 2013 was *Philomena*. It's based on the true story of Philomena Lee, an Irish young woman who gave birth to a son out of wedlock in 1952. As a Catholic in Ireland in the 1950s, Philomena was sent to a convent, where she gave birth to her son. For four years, she worked in the kitchen at the convent and cared for her son. She loved her little son very much. But one day, without her knowledge, the nuns gave her son up for adoption to a wealthy US couple. Philomena was crushed and angry.

Flash forward 50 years. Philomena was living in England and wished to find her long-lost son. British journalist Martin Sixsmith agreed to help in her search so that he might write her story for publication. The search began.

The search led Philomena and Martin to the US. Eventually they discovered that her son had died. The story did not end there. Philomena wished to find out as much as she could about him. So the pair traveled around the country, looking for people who knew her son, who might be able to tell her how his life turned out. The search was frustrating with many dead ends. At one point, they were driving through the countryside, and Philomena, who had remained a devout Catholic throughout her life, wanted to stop at a church. She wanted to go to confession because she felt that it would comfort her.

This was just too much for Martin, who was irreligious. His rising anger recounted for Philomena all the reasons why an intelligent person would not believe in God. He brought up a satirical headline

> Job discovered that God and his ways are a mystery.

in a newspaper he had recently read. The article described an earthquake in Turkey that left thousands of people dead. The headline read, "God Outdoes Terrorists Yet Again." Martin said, "Why God feels the need to wipe out hundreds of thousands of innocent people escapes me." He challenged Philomena, "You should ask them about that while you're in there." He was fond of her but viewed her as being somewhat simpleminded. As she left to go to confession, he suggested, "They'll probably say God moves in mysterious ways."

Martin Sixsmith is where Job was and where so many people remain. They conclude that the idea of God is for simpleminded people and is useless in our world of pain and misery. But Job discovered that God and his ways are a mystery. It seems to me that this is what sticks in the skeptics' craw most of all. They ask questions and want you to explain God to them. They believe God has to explain himself to them. If you can't, if you tell them that he is a mystery, then they reject him. End of story.

> "If God could be understood, then he is not God."

But the fact remains that God *is* a mystery. He is not completely explainable. St. Augustine once said, "If God could be understood, then he is not God." If God was understandable to us, he would just be like another human being. On the other hand, if he is the Creator of every molecule in our immeasurable universe, if he can put together all the complex life-forms of this world, including us humans, he is beyond our understanding. That is the answer God gave to Job. God asked, "Where were you when I laid the earth's foundation?" (Job 38:4). God never reveals everything about himself. We simply cannot understand it all. As Paul said in Romans 11:34, "Who has known the mind of the Lord?" Paul also said, "How unsearchable his judgments, and his paths beyond tracing out!" (Romans 11:33).

God is beyond us, just as we are higher and more complex than ants. Just as an ant with its tiny ant brain cannot completely understand a human being looming above it, so also we with our puny human brainpower cannot understand the God who made everything and filled the universe. There must be another way to look at what God tells us about himself. What can we learn to give us comfort and strength to go on in the face of troubles?

Another perspective on God's silence

I have wrestled with questions about the mystery of God's will and why we suffer while under the care of a loving God. I once found a helpful essay. It was one of the most enlightening things

I have ever read about God. John Schaller wrote it in 1916, originally in German, but later it was translated into English. The essay is titled "The Hidden God." It suggests another way of looking at the mysteries and questions we all have of God.

It is important to consider two important thoughts when looking at our questions of God. The first is to remember how much God has revealed to us in the Bible. Let me quote a bit from the essay on this point. John Schaller wrote:

> First . . . remember how much God has revealed to us in the Bible.

In the Holy Scriptures we enjoy the possession of God's revelation. There God has given us information about what he thinks of man, who enters the world as a sinner. There God sketches man for us, shows us how he sees [the sinner], and shares with us how he must deal with such creatures in his eternal righteousness. To make us eternally happy, God has further revealed the full riches of his love and mercy, according to which he has from eternity determined the salvation of the whole world of sinners and has accomplished it through his own Son in time. In his Word, God also announces to us how a sinner comes to possess this salvation and thus can be saved eternally. Besides these important items of divine revelation, the Bible also contains much information about God's nature, his will, and his dealings. We could never exhaust the riches of this revelation in our preaching, or even comprehend it in our own thoughts. (John Schaller, "Der Verborgene Gott," translated by J. Jeske, Wisconsin Lutheran Seminary essay files)

In other words, God reveals to us an amazing amount of information in the Bible. He tells us who he is. He tells us who we are. He tells us how we can go to heaven, which is through trust in his Son, Jesus, as our Savior. He reveals how he wants us to

> The second . . . God does not reveal everything to us.

live our lives. He makes powerful promises of forgiveness for all our sins and gives us hope for the life without pain and misery after this life is over.

The second important thought is that God does not reveal everything to us. Schaller continued:

Yet the expression, "God has been revealed," occurs only twice in the Holy Scriptures! And in both cases we notice immediately that the expression does not mean that God has revealed himself to men completely, that without any reservation he has unveiled his essence, will and works. . . . This truth was recognized by those enlightened men of God [that is, the prophets and apostles] to whom God granted his revelation. The Holy Ghost had enlightened Paul, so that he possessed the full measure of the revealed knowledge of God. And yet Paul realized the incompleteness of even this revelation, for he wrote: "Now I know in part" (1 Cor 13:12). . . . He could penetrate into God's secrets only so far, and no further. Isaiah once gave expression to the same realization . . . "Truly you are a God who hides himself, O God and Savior of Israel!" (Is 45:15). The same God who through prophets and apostles gave us revelations concerning his being and his will; the same God who in Jesus Christ himself became man and as the God-man draws ever so close to us—this revealed God remains at the same time *a hidden God*!

In other words, God does not reveal everything to us. In fact, he reveals only what we need to know as we journey through life here. Much about him is hidden—often the reasons behind some of his actions. This will always vex the Martin Sixsmiths of the world, but it is what the Bible says.

When we put these two thoughts together, another thought comes to mind. This idea makes sense to us most of the time, but when we add cancer and its suffering, an earthquake in Turkey, or a thousand other tragedies, we still wonder why. We pursue explanations. We want them. When they are not available, we are bewildered and refuse to accept that there is no explanation. Consider one excerpt from Schaller:

> But man is unwilling to let that truth stand. . . . [All aberrations] stem from a denial of the proposition that God is a hidden God, a God who cannot be grasped and understood by human reason. But people are not satisfied with what God has told us about himself; they want to go beyond that. . . . They speak of God's person and works in greater detail than the Scripture does. They don't want God to remain a hidden God.

In other words, when we refuse to accept that God is a hidden God, we look for reasonable explanations and say more about God than he has revealed about himself. Once we accept our own answers, we will inevitably believe and say wrong things about God. We may even conclude that what we think overshadows what God has revealed to humanity about Jesus, his forgiveness, and the promises of eternal life.

I think this was the main mistake of Job's friends. They did not believe that God was a hidden God. In the context of Job's situation, they thought God was easily explained: God punished the wicked. The reason people suffer was because they did something wicked. Job was suffering. Therefore, Job's friends concluded that it was the result of his sin. In that thinking, they lost the idea of a gracious, loving, and forgiving God. Job had not. He believed he was innocent, forgiven because of the Savior who would eventually come. Job even firmly confessed his faith in the Redeemer who would come and raise his scarred and broken body one day (Job 19:23-27). Yet God had not explained why he suffered. God had his own reasons that Job did not understand, which were never revealed to Job or his friends.

Job's friends said more about God than God had revealed, and they were wrong. That was why God rebuked them at the end of the book and told them, "You have not spoken the truth about me" (Job 42:8).

Yet Job still wondered why his question was not answered. He was not content to let God remain hidden. Job lamented his pain, which was perfectly understandable. He would like God to explain to him what was going on. For example, in Job 13:3, Job said, "I desire to speak to the Almighty and to argue my case with God." After a while he expressed the desire that he could present his case before God and God should have to explain himself to Job: "Let the Almighty answer me; let my accuser put his indictment in writing" (31:35). Now Job was on shaky ground. He was not willing to let God remain hidden. Eventually he said that God had wronged him as if he were in a court of law: "Know that God has wronged me" (19:6) and "As surely as God lives, who has denied me justice" (27:2). All this was understandable, but Job had gone too far. He accused God of not being loving or just. But God clearly revealed that he is fair and just: "The LORD is a God of justice" (Isaiah 30:18, among many other passages). We have learned from the New Testament that God is love (1 John 4:8,16). In Job's pain and frustration, he was unwilling to let the truth stand that God remained hidden about some things. He challenged it.

> In Job's pain and frustration, he was unwilling to let the truth stand that God remained hidden about some things. He challenged it.

Elihu

A fourth friend sat quietly listening to the other three. I haven't said too much about Elihu, but after 29 chapters of silence, Elihu spoke for 6 chapters (Job 32–37). In my humble opinion, Elihu pretty much said the same things as the other three friends, although he seemed much more concerned about Job personally. Unlike the first three friends, for example, Elihu actually addressed Job by name. He also emphasized that God had a purpose in Job's suffering, which was to lead Job to repentance and closer to God. However, Elihu ended up like the first three: saying more about God than what had been revealed to him. He was not satisfied with God being a hidden God.

But Elihu finally got at one of the truths of Job's story. In the next to last verse of Elihu's speech, he said, "The Almighty is beyond our reach and exalted in power [that is, he is hidden]; in his justice and great righteousness, he does not oppress" (Job 37:23). That is, no matter what happens, we cannot say that God is unjust or unloving. He does not oppress, and there must be another way to look at suffering, pain, and God's almighty control for all things.

And that is the point of God's words at the end of the book. He was saying, "I am a hidden God. I reveal to you so much and no more. You need to be content with that." Ultimately, the message of the book of Job is that God does not answer all our questions, just as my orthopedic doctor did not answer all my questions at my first visit with him and cancer doctors cannot always answer the questions of their patients or if the treatment they recommend will work as they think it will.

In Job's suffering, God asked Job to submit to him as the hidden God and trust in his power, justice, and love. Trust that he is the almighty God—that is the point of all the rhetorical questions from Job chapters 38–41. Trust that he is just and loving, as Elihu said in Job 37:23 and the Bible says over and over again in its pages.

And at the end of the story, that is what Job did. He did not abandon the love of God, who forgave him and would send the Redeemer to call him from his grave to eternal life.

God is still hidden

Let me return to Schaller's essay once more:

> Every child of God must also learn the lesson which once caused Job so much grief, and that is that even in his dealings with his own children God is a hidden God. . . . The ungodly prosper; they enjoy complete satisfaction in life; misfortunes do not seem to touch them. . . . By contrast, the godly man is no stranger to suffering. Everything seems to happen to him. He knows what it is to do without; tears are his constant companion. This is the picture which the psalmists have painted for us in colors drawn from their own experience, and every Christian knows that these are not rare exceptions which the psalmists describe. [It is] a common complaint of God's children.

As Job had to learn that God is a hidden God, so do we. And that's a good thing. We will actually be more content when we learn to be at peace with God, who does hide some things from us. We are not left without hope and comfort. Instead, we find comfort in the many things God has clearly revealed to us—and he has revealed many comforting messages in his Word. When we confront what our loving, hidden God has not revealed to us, we should trust that it is something we don't need to know. We trust that he knows best. When we are going through cancer, this is not easy, of course. All earthly signs indicate that a loving God is not in control of our lives. But faith in that almighty and loving God clings to his promises even when we cannot tell how those promises will be fulfilled.

> Every child of God must also learn the lesson which once caused Job so much grief . . . even in his dealings with his own children God is a hidden God.

Chapter 10
LESSONS TO LEARN FROM JOB

The book of Job teaches us, perhaps more than any other book of the Bible, that God is a hidden God. He reveals much to us but not everything. He answers many of our questions but not all of them. What he has shared with us in his Word is his love, forgiveness, and promise of eternal life. In these blessings we find endless comfort, strength, and hope. Therefore, we must find our comfort in the things he reveals to us.

I find there is something else about the book of Job that, I believe, is helpful to cancer patients, their loved ones, their friends, their fellow church members, and maybe even their pastors. Not only is God hidden to us, but we are also hidden to one another sometimes. We even hide from the way cancer influences our attitudes and thinking. Allow me to explain.

An incomprehensible mingling of faith and despair

Life is a roller coaster under normal circumstances. Sometimes things are going great. Work is satisfying. We feel productive. Our family life is tranquil and brings us happiness. Friends, recreation, and free time are welcome diversions. At other times work is frustrating, maybe even depressing. Things are strained at home. There are problems in our relationships with our

As a cancer patient, does this roller coaster seem even more herky-jerky? One day: peaceful acceptance. The next: fear, anger, questions.

spouse or children. No recreation or diversion seems to relieve the tension. And the roller coaster goes up and down in our emotions as well. One day we are at peace. The next we feel turmoil. I think we all are familiar with this situation.

As a cancer patient, does this roller coaster seem even more herky-jerky? One day: peaceful acceptance. The next: fear, anger, questions. I think that Christians sometimes feel guilty about this. "If I was a good Christian, then I should always have peace in my heart," so the thinking goes. "I should accept what comes from the Lord's hand without grumbling or complaining. Doesn't the Bible say that somewhere?"

When I look at the conversation between Job and his friends, I think it is often hard to follow. The main reason is that Job was all over the place—like a roller coaster. In one place he said one thing; in another place he seemed to say something altogether different. Even at the end of the book, God rebuked Job but then commended him. It leads to questions: "What was going on in Job's heart? Did he trust in God? Did he see God as his friend or only as his tormentor?"

The answer is both. And I think that is comforting.

> Our lives and emotions certainly seem like a roller coaster at times.

Our lives and emotions certainly seem like a roller coaster at times. That's true for everyone. For Christians, a new dimension is added to what everyone else feels and thinks. When we become Christians, we have faith and hope in the promises of a loving God. Our faith clings to those promises in the ups and downs of life, but we still have a sinful flesh that opposes our faith and trust in God and tugs at us to move us away from him and his promises.

The apostle Paul wrote about the conflict between faith and the sinful nature in two places. In Galatians he wrote, "The flesh desires what is contrary to the Spirit, and the Spirit what is contrary to the flesh. They are in conflict with each other" (Galatians 5:17). He also wrote about it in the familiar passages from Romans chapter 7, "I do not understand what I do. For what I want to do I do not do, but what I hate I do. I know that good itself does not dwell in me, that is, in my sinful nature. For I have the desire to do what is good, but I cannot carry it out. Although I want to do good, evil is right there with me. For in my inner being I delight in God's law; but I see another law at work in me, waging war against the law of my mind" (Romans 7:15,18,21-23). Paul found the remedy for this "war" in the gospel. He wrote, "Thanks be to God, who delivers me through Jesus Christ our Lord!" (Romans 7:25).

What does this all mean to cancer patients? They bring this struggle along with them in their pain, questions, surgeries, and chemotherapy. Job was all over the place. So are they. Job had serious questions about God as he challenged him and wanted to know why he suffered. Yet Job expressed confidence and hope in God, the Redeemer to come, and the promise of the resurrection and victory over death. I think Christian cancer patients also feel the tension, and their loved ones do too. Both the patients and their loved ones anguish over it.

As I prepared to write the book, I returned to an essay I read long ago that was written about Job by August Pieper, a seminary professor from 1902-1941. He commented:

> What an incomprehensible mingling of faith and unbe-lief, of despair and trust (in the heart of Job)! If Jere-miah 17:9 is true of natural man ("The heart is deceitful above all things and beyond cure. Who can understand it?"), then the heart of the Christian . . . is all the more an unsolvable mystery. The psychology of him who is enduring temptation will moreover, ever remain a deep mystery in us. (August Pieper, "The Book of Job in its Significance for Preaching and the Care of Souls,"

translated by Tom Jeske, Wisconsin Lutheran Seminary essay files)

> We experience "an incomprehensible mingling . . . of despair and trust."

The struggle for Christians may be tame in everyday, normal life. We feel the temptations to turn from our Lord, but we quickly come back to his promises and resist. But often it is not that simple. When we face serious temptations that lead us to doubt God's care and his promises, we struggle—one day (perhaps even one minute) turning to God in faith and then the next day or minute screaming anger at him. We experience "an incomprehensible mingling . . . of despair and trust." Our heart is "an unsolvable mystery." This was true of Job. I think it is also true of many Christian cancer patients.

Let's explore some examples of Job's struggle with his suffering and God's promises. Maybe you can relate.

God is too close to me/God is too far away from me

Job said to God, "What is mankind that you make so much of them, that you give them so much attention, that you examine them every morning and test them every moment? Will you never look away from me, or let me alone even for an instant? If I have sinned, what have I done to you, you who see everything we do? Why have you made me your target?" (Job 7:17-20). He lamented that it was as if God was stalking him and watching his every move, ready to punish him for the slightest sin. These questions did not come from faith in a loving God. They came, instead, from a heart that wanted to hide from God.

But then Job lamented, "Why do you hide your face?" (Job 13:24). He also wanted to find God for comfort and solace. He declared, "If only I knew where to find him; if only I could go to his dwelling! If I go to the east, he is not there; if I go to the west, I do not find him. When he is at work in the north, I do not see him; when he turns to the south, I catch no glimpse of him" (Job 23:3,8,9). He yearned for God as all those who trust in him do in their distress.

Cancer sufferer, do you sometimes feel like God is on your back, stalking and punishing you for some unknown wrongdoing? But then does God seem distant sometimes? Where is he? Why doesn't he tell you what's going on? You want his comfort, but you cannot feel his presence. Job experienced that same conflicting cauldron of emotions.

> Do you sometimes feel like God is on your back, stalking and punishing you for some unknown wrongdoing?

I want to talk to God/It wouldn't do any good anyway

Sometimes Job proclaimed his urgent desire to confront God, talk to him, and argue with him, wanting God to explain himself. Here is one of the clearest examples: "Let the Almighty answer me; let my accuser put his indictment in writing" (Job 31:35). If you are suffering, you probably relate to this desire: "God, could you please just explain everything to me? I'm so angry and frustrated at your silence."

But Job also held a clear picture of his status with God. He was a sinner who deserved nothing from God: "How then can I dispute with him? I do not believe he would give me a hearing. Who can challenge him?" (Job 9:14,16,19). "I can't confront God. He isn't going to explain himself to me, and he doesn't owe me an explanation." Can you relate to this stoic resignation?

I wish I had a helper/I know I do

At one point Job complained, "If only there were someone to mediate between us, someone to bring us together, someone to remove God's rod from me, so that his terror would frighten me no more. Then I would speak up without fear of him, but as it now stands with me, I cannot" (Job 9:33-35). He said that if only he had someone, like a lawyer, to go between him and God, to plead his case for him, to represent him before God—then everything would be okay. "Oh, if only I had such a helper," Job cried for mercy. Isn't that what we all need? Someone to bring us close to God—especially when we are suffering and feel so distant from him. Job lamented that he didn't feel like he had such a helper.

But in the most beautiful parts of the book, Job expressed that he had just such a helper. He confidently proclaimed, "Even now my witness is in heaven; my advocate is on high. My intercessor is my friend as my eyes pour out tears to God; on behalf of a man he pleads with God as one pleads for a friend" (Job 16:19-21). Job had faith in God's mercy. Job claimed that he knew he had someone to represent him before God. He put his confidence in the advocate on high.

In the most memorable verses of the book, Job confessed his faith, "I know that my redeemer lives, and that in the end he will stand on the earth. And after my skin has been destroyed, yet in my flesh I will see God; I myself will see him with my own eyes—I, and not another. How my heart yearns within me!" (Job 19:25-27).

From our perspective, as people who have the entire Bible, we know that this Advocate and Redeemer whom Job wanted is none other than our Savior, Jesus. Thousands of years after Job, Jesus would come and live a perfect life in Job's place and die on the cross to pay for all of Job's sins, just as he has done for all of us. Job knew the promises that a Savior would come, and he found comfort in those promises in the midst of his suffering. The apostle John confirmed the faith of Job: "We have an advocate with the Father—Jesus Christ, the Righteous One" (1 John 2:1) and "Because I live, you also will live" (John 14:19).

Yet sometimes Job was in deep despair, as if he found no comfort in his Savior at all.

How could this be?

Remember the quote from August Pieper? He suggested that "an incomprehensible mingling of faith and unbelief, of despair and trust" is in the hearts of suffering believers. Believers, more than most people, ride a roller coaster of emotions. It can be "an unsolvable mystery" to those who know them and even to themselves. Job was a believer. He still trusted in God as his help. He still trusted in the future Savior. But at the same time, unbelief and despair waged war against the faith in his heart. God knew that underneath Job's complaints was still a man of faith, and that was why God commended Job at the end.

God knows your heart too

I think that if you are a cancer sufferer, this is a comforting thought. I think that if you are a loved one, a friend, a fellow church member, or a pastor of a cancer sufferer, this is instructive. The heart of the suffering believer may indeed be like "an unsolvable mystery" because of its "incomprehensible mingling of faith and unbelief, of despair and trust."

Fear and anxiety

Because of this mingling, Christians who have cancer experience thoughts and emotions that might lead them to question their faith. One of them is fear—sometimes called anxiety. Remember what Lisa said when she found out about her cancer: "When the diagnosis came, I realized how weak and terrified I was. It knocked me to my knees." Lisa dealt with a lot of fear during her cancer treatment, and of course, like all cancer patients, she always has the nagging fear that it will come back. There were, and occasionally still are, a lot of fears. Lisa echoed Job's comment. One of the first things Job said in

> Christians who have cancer experience thoughts and emotions that might lead them to question their faith.

his conversation with his friends was "What I *feared* has come upon me; what I *dreaded* has happened to me. I have no peace, no quietness; I have no rest, but only turmoil" (Job 3:25,26, emphasis added).

For most people, Christians included, cancer brings fear. Fear of what? Let's start with the obvious: fear of dying. If you are diagnosed with late-stage cancer or any stage of cancer, it's pretty hard not to think about death. We can say whatever we want in our Sunday morning Bible class about how we, as Christians, can face death with joy because we know we will be in heaven. But for most of us, when the reality of death stares us in the face, it's scary. There is fear and there are tears. Death is a scary thing because God did not create us to die originally. Death entered this world. God had threatened Adam and Eve with death if they disobeyed and sinned. You are afraid of the pain and process of dying. You are afraid of the unknown. You are afraid of how your death will affect your spouse and children.

But maybe at the same time you wonder, "Aren't Christians supposed to face death with a faith like Paul's, who said in Philippians 1:23, 'I desire to depart and be with Christ'? If I die, I know I will be with Jesus in perfect happiness in heaven. What kind of Christian am I if I don't have the same fearless, joyfully expectant attitude toward death that Paul had?" Those questions reveal the mingling of fear and faith.

There are other fears, such as the fear of the pain of treatment. That pain is all too real. In the face of cancer, we find financial fear: "I'm going to lose income if I have to miss a lot of time from work. How am I going to pay for all these bills?" Navigating through hospital bills and insurance forms can beat the Christian charity and optimism out of anyone. But Christians aren't supposed to be afraid. Didn't Jesus say so in the Sermon on the Mount? "Do not worry about tomorrow" (Matthew 6:34). We are supposed to present a courageous face to our family, fellow church members, and neighbors. Why are we so afraid?

What we experience at such a time is the "incomprehensible mingling of faith and unbelief, of despair and trust."

Anger

Another emotion at odds with faith is anger. It is easy to become impatient and angry with many people. Let's admit it: It's easy to become angry with God. It's hard to understand what God has in mind when a man dies of cancer and leaves behind a husbandless wife, fatherless children, or grandfatherless grandchildren. This is difficult to square with our belief in a loving God. With despairing Job, cancer patients and their loved ones ask, "Why, God, why?"

As cancer patients go through their ordeal, they get angry with other people, including those close to them—even God himself. I was a parish pastor for only six years. I served two small congregations that I loved dearly. I ministered to more people than I can remember who were dying of cancer, and then I preached at their funerals. I remember that on at least two occasions I received interesting requests before preaching a funeral sermon for someone who had died of cancer. The children of the deceased would come to me and say something like this: "Pastor, it may surprise you, but as Mom suffered from cancer these past months (or years), at times she could be pretty hard on Dad. We would really appreciate it if in your funeral sermon you would mention how hard it was on him and how patient he was with Mom." I gathered from those conversations that a person dying of cancer is sometimes difficult with loved ones. But a Christian husband or wife would never be difficult on his or her spouse, right?

> As cancer patients go through their ordeal, they get angry with other people, including those close to them—even God himself.

Job was sometimes sarcastic with his friends: "How you have helped the powerless! What great insight you have displayed!"

(Job 26:2,3). Can suffering people become snippy even to those who love them? Of course they can as they struggle with their pain, fears, and exhaustion. Their Christian patience can be worn thin. We note here too the struggle of faith and love with rage and anger.

If you have cancer, it's painful, sad, and overwhelming. The fact of the matter is that much of the time you feel terrible. So you are gloomy. You complain. If you're a Christian, sometimes you get depressed about how you're dealing with your cancer, not just the cancer itself. The Bible says, "Rejoice in the Lord always. I have learned the secret of being content in any and every situation. I can do all this through him who gives me strength" (Philippians 4:4,12,13). Yet most of the time you don't feel joyful. You don't feel content. You don't feel like a conqueror. You just feel like crap. Christians aren't supposed to feel that way, right?

> What "an incomprehensible mingling of faith and unbelief, of despair and trust." That was Job's heart. That's our heart also.

One of the messages of Job is that faith and despair exist side by side in the heart of the sufferer, and this despair can show itself in a number of different actions. Don't beat yourself up for that. Find deliverance, forgiveness, peace, and love in your Savior. It may last only a short time, but turn to the advocate, the giver of life. What "an incomprehensible mingling of faith and unbelief, of despair and trust." That was Job's heart. That's our heart also.

Loved ones need to remember this too

All of this is, I think, instructive for family members and friends and maybe even pastors of cancer patients. Don't interpret words of fear as a denial of faith in the promises of heaven. Don't interpret anger, even anger with God, as a denial of confidence in the love of God. Don't interpret persistent gloominess as a lack of faith, since faith means you should be optimistic. When your family member or friend is difficult to live with, it is not the time to question the sincerity of his or her Christian life. It is the time for you to dig deep and show Christlike patience and mercy.

Faith and despair live side by side in the heart of the Christian sufferer. God knew that was true for Job. One of the problems of Job's friends was that they did not understand this.

> Faith and despair
> live side by side
> in the heart of the
> Christian sufferer.

Of course, Job's friends had a lot of problems. Let's talk about that next.

Chapter 11

FOR LOVED ONES, FRIENDS, AND PASTORS

Try not to be like Job's friends

This book is for two groups of people: cancer patients (Group One) and their loved ones, friends, and pastors (Group Two). Job's friends "heard about all the troubles" and came to "sympathize with him and comfort him" (Job 2:11). We have already noted that their efforts to help were not very helpful. While learning from the story of Job, we also can learn some lessons from his friends. Job's friends thought they were being comforting, but their words accomplished the opposite. Instead of comforting Job, these friends just irritated and frustrated him.

Eliphaz-, Bildad-, and Zophar-like comfort or, rather, no comfort

One of the most serious flaws in the comfort of Job's friends is that they did not understand God. They thought of God like an umpire who awarded his blessings based on his subjects' behavior. They thought Job deserved his woes because he had done something to offend God. They directed Job to repent so he could make himself acceptable to the almighty, majestic God of the universe. Job claimed he was innocent. He understood that

> One of the most serious flaws in the comfort of Job's friends is that they did not understand God.

God is a God of undeserved love and blessings—a God of grace, not a God of rewards for good behavior. When all these troubles descended on Job, he proclaimed, "The LORD gave and the LORD has taken away; may the name of the LORD be praised" (Job 1:21). God declared Job innocent because of the Redeemer who was to come. Yet Job did not understand why he suffered. He wrestled with the reasons behind God's will. On the other hand, his friends did not understand the reasons either but from a much different perspective—the principle of reward and punishment.

Both Job and his friends struggled with why people suffer. Job's friends never abandoned their thinking that people are often responsible for their own misery because bad choices bring bad results. However, Job's troubles were not the result of his bad choices. Instead he had been blessed by a loving God. Then God took away all those blessings. Why? God hid the answer. Job's friends did not agree. They thought that Job must have done some dark secret sin that deserved his troubles. Yet Job did not desert God because he didn't understand the answer to his question. Job's friends turned against Job. His wife said, "Curse God and die!" (Job 2:9). Job refused. He would not desert the God of grace who promised resurrection from death (Job 19:23-27). Job had to continue to believe in the God of love even if he didn't understand. His friends offered what they thought was comfort, but none of it was comforting.

> I think the one lesson you can learn from Job is that God continues to love you.

If you recently have been diagnosed with cancer and are stepping into that scary, dark cave of treatment, I think the one lesson you can learn from Job is that God continues to love you. But this is a very difficult thing to learn. Many of the people around you can lift you up, but they can also bring you down hard. Lisa would wholeheartedly agree with that, since that was her experience too.

People can be insensitive, even when they don't realize it. Their words and thoughts are different from Job's friends but no better at giving comfort. One acquaintance, upon seeing my wife in her headscarf looking like a cancer patient going through chemotherapy, asked, "So how much time has the doctor given you to live?" I think even Eliphaz, Bildad, and Zophar would have been more tactful.

A young woman going through treatment for Hodgkin's lymphoma occasionally heard the comment "Oh, you're lucky! You have the good kind of cancer." Not really comforting. When you have cancer, you do not consider yourself lucky, and I don't think there's any such thing as a good kind of cancer.

Sometimes when we talk to people going through something hard, we feel the need to share with them all our similar experiences. We say, "This reminds me of when I had . . ." We feel the need to tell them about everyone we know who has gone through something similar. I contend that this is usually not helpful. Telling cancer patients about all your friends and relatives with cancer and how many of them suffered or died is not going to lift their spirits. It will probably accomplish the opposite.

I don't know where all the information on the internet about cancer comes from, but there sure is a lot of it. And there is no end of advice for cancer patients. There is no end of information about what causes cancer, not all of it substantiated. If someone has cancer and his or her friends read that this particular product or that particular food causes cancer, these friends wander into the thinking of Job's friends. They want to be helpful, but they tell their friend with cancer to avoid that product or food. The cancer patient is hearing, "If you just had been smart enough to avoid these cancer-causers, then you wouldn't be in the boat you are in now. Trouble comes because you didn't do what you should have done."

These helpful people certainly have no malice in their hearts and are just trying to be good friends, but to the cancer sufferer it might come across as unintentionally accusatory. Just as Job's friends thought they were being helpful when they really weren't, our words might have the same uncomforting effect.

Proverbs of ashes

When I asked current or former cancer patients for examples of comfort that weren't really comforting, the first thing they mentioned almost every time was the spiritual comfort that came across as empty platitudes. Eliphaz, Bildad, and Zophar eventually became mean-spirited in their comments to Job. I don't think these modern spiritual encouragements are ever offered from a hurtful spirit, but they often come across as empty platitudes. Job called them "proverbs of ashes" (Job 13:12). Here are some examples.

> Examples of comfort that weren't really comforting . . .

"You'll get through this. God will help you."

This is true and biblical in a way. But when people's bodies have been wracked with the debilitating pain of chemotherapy and their spirits with the fear of what the future holds—they just don't feel strong in body or spirit—such words can feel a little shallow and vaguely cheerleaderish. These words can come across a little like an unintentional accusation. "You have the power to get through this with God's help." These sufferers don't feel like they are getting through it. Like Job, God feels distant from them. They don't feel his help. If these words are offered without really listening to the cancer sufferer's situation, they come across like the words of Job's friends. Even though much of what the friends told Job about God was true, their words came across as "proverbs of ashes."

"God will bring you closer to him through this."

Who can argue with that? We know from the Bible and personal experience that God often uses our afflictions to bring us closer to his promises. We learn to treasure those promises more in our troubles. The apostle Paul taught us that in 2 Corinthians chapter 12. God had afflicted him with a "thorn in the flesh" (2 Corinthians 12:7). Paul pleaded for it to be taken away, but God told him, "My grace is sufficient for you, for my power is made perfect in weakness" (2 Corinthians 12:9). In this weakness, Paul learned how to lean on God and his strength. Surely, that is a true and comforting biblical lesson.

But once again, if these words are spoken without real empathy, they sound empty. Remember that the number one mistake Job's friends made was claiming to understand God and his ways when, in fact, God's ways are often hidden from

> If these words are spoken without real empathy, they sound empty.

his people. They refused to accept that God is a hidden God. They failed to understand why a loving God sends troubles for his own reasons and doesn't explain why. Sometimes we are guilty of claiming the same understanding of God and his ways. We simply do not know what God will bring through a person's suffering because of cancer. Beware of "proverbs of ashes."

"We've been Romans 8:28'd to death."

A great blessing of my life is that I get to teach the book of Romans every year in my junior religion class. Every year I get to teach the beautiful second half of Romans chapter 8, arguably the most comforting portion of the Bible. I think many Christians would vote for Romans 8:28 as the most comforting passage of God's Word: "We know that in all things God works for the good of those who love him." This passage tells us that even in bad and painful experiences, God will bring some kind of blessing. As Christians who know that we have a good and gracious God "who did not spare his own Son, but gave him up for us all" (Romans 8:32), we know that God can and does bring good out of evil. We have all experienced many examples of this.

But even this precious passage can be uncomforting.

I was teaching a Bible class on Romans chapter 8 one Sunday morning. The class members were discussing how this chapter is so comforting and especially verse 28. An insightful man in the class shared something he had heard recently at a Christian men's retreat: A pastor's wife had died, so the pastor and his children heard many comforting words from loving friends and family members. But after a while, one of the children said, "I feel like we've been Romans 8:28'd to death."

I think the point is that even the most comforting biblical words fall short of being comforting when you hear them over and over again. It becomes numbing. You feel that people are just saying the words and talking past you. They aren't really thinking about what you are going through. In order for any words to truly be comforting, even God's inspired and powerful words, they need to be accompanied by real sympathy and empathy.

"This is all part of God's plan."

During my senior year at the seminary, my class and I studied Romans for the entire year. When discussing Romans chapter 8, the professor taught something I don't think I had heard before (or if I did learn it, I hadn't really absorbed it). I remember that the professor cautioned against saying, "This is God's will" or "This is all part of God's plan," when comforting people who were suffering the effects of sin in this sin-cursed world. We know that God will do his will in this world and that he has good plans for us. In Jeremiah 29:11 God says, "I know the plans I have for you, . . . plans to prosper you and not to harm you, plans to give you hope and a future." What we do know is that God loves us even in the worst of times. He demonstrated that love when he sent his Son, Jesus. By Jesus' suffering and death for us, God declared us

> We don't always know what the will of God is.

holy and innocent, and by Jesus' resurrection from the grave, God promised us victory over death too. And we know that he will work for our good in all things as Romans 8:28 says. But we don't always know what the will of God is. We don't always know what his plans are. We don't always know how God will work for good until much later. Beware of saying more than what God has revealed in his Word.

This was a big reason why the comfort of Job's friends was, in reality, not comfort. The friends claimed to know why God had allowed the suffering of Job. They never turned to God's love for Job and all humanity. "Why do we suffer?" They didn't really know the reason, yet they claimed to know God's will and plans. They didn't really know what God's will was in Job's situation or the plans God had for him. They said more than what God had revealed to them.

Pointing cancer patients and their families to God's plan may be highly depressing and frustrating. This comfort is difficult for those who are suffering from cancer or whose loved ones suffer or have died from cancer. "This is part of God's plan," we tell them. "Really? It's God's will for me or my spouse to suffer intensely? Really? It's God's plan for this child to suffer from leukemia and go through excruciating chemotherapy? Really? It's God's will for a young man to die of cancer and leave behind a widow and fatherless children?" The fact of the matter is that we do not know if it is God's will and plan or simply a by-product of the frustrated, sin-cursed world we live in.

We know that God will work for good in all things because that's what Romans 8:28 says. He will work for good even when things seem to be different from his love. But the Bible never tells us that we will exactly know all of God's plans for us in this life. The Bible never tells us that God will reveal to us his exact will in everything. Sometimes we can see what the plan was years after the fact. Maybe we will only understand it when we are in heaven. God never let Job know the answer while Job was on earth. Even after Job was blessed again as he was before his suffering, he may have wondered why God did what he did. Beware of the error of Job's friends. Beware of saying more than God really reveals.

A personal perspective

My cousin Laura and her family have suffered through many trials. Her beloved children have gone through more health challenges than you could imagine. It would take a whole other book to tell you everything that this wonderfully strong and patient Christian family has endured. Probably the heaviest burden is that the youngest child, Katie, has suffered painful and debilitating epileptic seizures throughout her life. This has required endless procedures, medications, trips to Children's Hospital, and delicate surgeries on her young brain.

Recently, as if Laura didn't have enough on her plate with all the medical needs of her family, she was diagnosed with breast cancer. Like Lisa, Laura also underwent a mastectomy and other treatment. Perhaps more than any person I have known, Laura can relate to the life of Job.

I'm sure Laura would be uncomfortable being praised in any way, but the fact of the matter is that not only does she bear up under the strain of what she has gone through, but she also lets the light of her faith shine brightly. She writes about her family's experience on her blog. The Holy Spirit has given her a wonderful ability to share God's strength and comfort through her writing. Although the lives of Laura and her family members have been difficult, I am constantly encouraged and lifted up by her faith, optimism, and insights.

Laura rarely ever seems to be complaining in her blog, but within months of this book's writing she shared two entries that I thought were very instructive. She wrote about how people say things to a cancer patient that they think are helpful, but they have the opposite effect. It struck me how similar this was to the experience of Job with his friends.

She wrote:

> So I once again have something to get off my chest. I too often feel like I'm in some sort of crap contest, but I have no desire to be in it, I have no entry nor ambition to win at such a contest. Let me elaborate please.
>
> Sometimes it seems that when a person has a lot of battles and hardships others with their own crud find you and I am totally cool with that. Let me tell you what I am NOT cool with. Sometimes random folks find out I had breast cancer, I briefly share a bit about it at their inquiry, NO PROB. I am not ashamed or embarrassed, but I often wander into a full out game of I can one up you with my cancer story. Out of nowhere a table and chairs seem to appear and I find myself with a hand of cards and the "opponent" has *their* cards and one by one they lay out card after card of "I had X number of chemo treatments, I had a DOUBLE mastectomy, I had . . ." You see where I'm going with this, right? Let me tell you right now what I do when this occurs and you can do what you wish, but I honestly feel for self-preservation and to keep in the spirit of Christ, I FOLD!!!!!!!! I don't want any part of any such "games" because, yes, in comparison to other folks my cancer journey was nowhere near as horrific, painful, or horrible perhaps, but WHO CARES!?!??! What really is the point of that other *person? Do they* need me to say, "You're way more awesome and strong than I am" Do they need me to say my cancer was NOTHING compared to theirs? What is that? I fold people, I FOLD.
>
> There was this time when I was in a store purchasing a bathing suit for my daughter for her birthday and somehow my cancer process came up with the cashier. I shared my experience briefly. Then she had the attitude like that's nothing and went on and on about HER cancer (multiple recurrences, multiple rounds of

chemo), and I seriously considered telling her, about my DAUGHTER'S trials—but I stopped myself, I FOLDED. I wished her well, told her I would pray for her and told myself, DON'T do that to anyone at any time because it is thoughtless, ridiculous and one of the least helpful things you can do to another person. I walked out of the store feeling like a moron like "What is my problem?" I should have zero issues with what I have endured, it's NOTHING compared to that woman. I felt like a wimp, a fool, a joke, a spoiled brat and ridiculous. But I'm not any of those things, not when my Lord's righteousness shines on me, so I should never allow myself to feel those things. I am chosen, I am loved, and my struggle is HIS struggle too and he never belittles me, he never compares my struggle to his. I'm not going to do that either!

Along the same lines I am going to be very blunt and honest. I also find it a bad call to say to me or anyone else who has hardships "I know this is nothing compared to what you are going through, but—" and then they share an issue they are personally struggling with. Please don't say this! It makes the hearer of this feel like we are in an elite group of people, the cream of the crap group, like our life is just a cesspool of horror and dismal junk. IT ISN'T!!!!!!!!!!!!!!! I am not interested in calculating who has it the worst. I am not at all going to spend time on [whose] struggle is quantitatively the absolute, honest to goodness, most trying and difficult. It is wasted time. Are there people who have it worse than me? YES, but again, I don't think I have it at all that bad. Am I honest that I struggle? Yes, because I am not going to whitewash anything. I wish to shine an honest light on epilepsy, congenital heart defects, HHT, cancer and anything else that may creep up in our life. It is a part of our life, but it is not our whole life, JESUS IS. I do NOT ever wish to shine a light on woe is me and say

I have a crap heap of a life. I DON'T, I have a blessed life. I have a full life. I have an abundant life, and it is ALL because of who I live for, who I serve, who I love—my Lord, my family and so many other folks in my life that I love as family.

I remembered my Lord's words. "But you are a chosen people, a royal priesthood, a holy nation, God's special possession, that you may declare the praises of him who called you out of darkness into his wonderful light. Once you were not a people, but now you are the people of God; once you had not received mercy, but now you have received mercy." (1 Peter 2:9-10) I have been able to declare God's goodness despite my struggle and I was chosen by God to do so, to proclaim him as awesome despite my struggle and to persevere and give him all the

> Interject and infuse the grace of God that was so freely given to you through blood that was shed willingly and unselfishly.

glory through it. I was NOT called to claim any of the glory for myself and I was not called to make others around me feel small and stupid because they are struggling with something "smaller" than my own struggle, my LORD NEVER did that. He hung on the cross and not ONCE does he look at us thinking or saying, your measly problems are NOTHING compared to what I endured. He NEVER SAYS IT, so why do we?????????

Do you have someone you brush shoulders with who is struggling with something? I don't care how big or small you perceive it to be. If *they* are struggling with it, it is BIG to them, so put your crud aside, please. I challenge you to just listen without comparing it to your own situation. I challenge you to NOT say, "Wow, and I thought I had problems." I challenge you to just be here, support as you are able and don't interject your own guilt or self-importance. Interject and infuse the grace of God that was so freely given to you through blood that was shed willingly and unselfishly. Be that person, be that grace-filled person. You don't have to go through the same thing as someone else to support them. You don't have to say the perfect thing. You don't have to be their everything. They already have a God who is that. They sometimes JUST need a hug and you can say, "I don't claim to know what you are feeling, but know I love you, I am here for you. And if you forget who you are in Christ because your heart is so very broken right now, I will be here to remind you how very much you are worth in him."

Thank you for all the prayers for me through all of this. Thank you for the support and words you have shared. I seriously can't tell you how much even a "tiny" means to our family. It means you are hearing us, praying for us, and carrying us in your hearts. THANK YOU!

The Lord is good and gracious, with his help let us boldly go among the broken and share his grace and mercy. There isn't a one of us who doesn't need it, even those that seem together, we all need our Savior's glue.

In another blog she wrote:

"For I am convinced that neither death nor life, neither angels nor demons, neither the present nor the future, nor any powers, neither height nor depth, nor anything else in all creation, will be able to separate us from the love of God that is in Christ Jesus our Lord." (Romans 8:38-39)

I have very little need to speak of anything regarding what I have gone through with my breast cancer. I don't bring it up to anyone other than occasionally my husband and it is mostly regarding an upcoming appointment. I have very few that ask me about it and that is fine by me. I know cancer is an uncomfortable subject and I had it in an uncomfortable to speak about it place. I respect this. I, however, need to tell you what I can [no longer] just be silent about because I can take it no more.

I am fully aware that my cancer journey has not remotely compared to many. I know that I am VERY blessed at the timely manner in which we caught it. I too have lost loved ones to cancer and fully know the extent in which it can ravage and own a person until there is very little of the person left. I honestly can say I have survivor's guilt. At times I talk to my Lord and say, why was my cancer more easily taken care of than some others, I don't deserve such mercy and grace. Most of the time I feel my cancer not worth mentioning, not worth having feelings about, not worth much of anything

> As soon as anyone hears the word cancer in respect to their health it is not nothing.

I will be blunt: I can't handle hearing even one more time "so nice, or so great, or you're so lucky, or so glad you didn't have to have chemo or radiation." Let me just say, I know this. Though I was ready to do both if that is how I was so directed, but yes, my cancer graciously didn't warrant it as it was small in size. Let me tell you right now, every time I hear this I actually hear "Your cancer was virtually nothing, so get over it, move on and who gives a rip." I know they may not mean this at all, but this is MOST definitely how the receiver of such words will take it who is in my shoes.

As soon as anyone hears the word cancer in respect to their health it is not nothing. When one's body is forever changed due to cancer, it is not nothing. When one is faced with their own mortality and had to go through multiple times waiting on test results to find out just how much cancer will impact your life, it is NOT nothing. It is very much something; I am very much not over it. I am very much still trying to find my feet. I am very much still playing catch up from my surgeries and feeling crummy . . .

So I am going to go ahead and live confidently in the fact that what I went through was the furthest thing from nothing. I am going to go ahead and not feel badly if I struggle from time to time with what I have gone through and continue to go through.

The fact is if I ran into someone who had a different kind of cancer than my own, I wouldn't know totally what to say either. The fact is nobody knows the right thing to say all the time, certainly not I. The fact remains however, that if we stop trying to understand another person's plight because we have blinders on because of our own experience with pain then just don't say a darn thing. If you're too wrapped up in your hurts don't go making someone else feel worse about feeling badly about their hurts they are struggling with just because you feel it isn't as struggle-worthy as your own plight. Be kind, or be quiet.

I forgive anyone who has hurt me, don't worry about that. My sinless Lord has done so to me countless times; how much more so should I do to my fellow sinners.

I, as I have said before, speak on behalf of all those who struggle, not just myself. I am in no way trying to make someone feel badly if they said the "wrong" thing (I have done so as well). I am simply trying to encourage empathy and kindness and reminding, though it is SO difficult, you can't really be helpful to another if you are

tangled up in your own hurt. Our God can use the hurting, and only through him can we put our hurts aside
from time to time to truly show his love to others who
are hurting alongside us.

So, you might be thinking,
Laura, what do I say to someone who is struggling with
cancer or something else? My
advice is think about what you
would want to hear. I person-
ally love it when someone randomly shares a Bible verse
with me. Check in with them from time to time, "been
thinking about you and wondering how you are, praying for you, here to listen if you need it." Remind them
of God's love, the passage I include here is such a beautiful reminder of just how unfathomable his love is for
us and even the most sizable of struggles and hurts will
not ever change that hugeness of his love for us. Try not
to compare (I personally know how hard this is) situa-
tions, even if you saw a parent, a spouse, a friend pass
away from cancer or something else horrible, use that
experience to understand the depth of someone else's
pain but with God's help don't let it cloud your judge-
ment and belittle another person's struggle. For myself
so often it wasn't the cancer itself that ate away at my
peace of mind it was the million other things that kept
prying at myself, the things I wasn't getting to, the time
I wanted to spend with some-
one or something but couldn't
because I didn't have it in me.

Above all, and this is kind of
where I am at presently, know
when you are too neck deep in
hurt that you have to step back
and let someone else do the

> My advice is think about what you would want to hear.

> Know when you are too neck deep in hurt that you have to step back and let someone else do the comforting.

comforting . . . The Lord's love will help this drowning
mama, he is lovingly helping you too. May we all be able
to look past our hurt and the Lord will help us find the
right words to comfort those we love.

Thank you, Laura, for helping me learn how not to be like Eliphaz, Bildad, and Zophar.

Chapter 12
SO WHAT SHOULD I DO?
WHAT SHOULD I SAY?

I have a fear after writing the previous chapters. My fear is that you, dear reader, will get the message that just about anything you say to a cancer sufferer is wrong. I don't want to paralyze the readers of this book with fear: "Any *helpful* thing I might say to my friend with cancer will not really be helpful, so I shouldn't say anything. Maybe I should just keep my mouth shut and stay away."

I certainly do not want that to be the message.

I'm also afraid that the previous pages might have given the impression that most of the people who tried to encourage Lisa and our family came across as uncomforting. Nothing could be further from the truth. Lisa received no end of comfort from our Christian friends and family. She and I will remember their kind words and deeds for the rest of our lives. Other cancer sufferers I have spoken with echo that sentiment.

> Lisa received no end of comfort from our Christian friends and family.

Yes, a Christian person who is suffering can be Romans 8:28'd to death. But what Romans 8:28 says is still true: God works for good in all things, even bad things like cancer. And I'm convinced that the number one good thing that God brings into the life of sufferers is the Christian love they receive from fellow believers.

Now a word in defense of Job's friends

One morning at school many years ago, we teachers were having our faculty Bible study. At the end of the hour, a coworker shared that a friend of his was in the hospital after attempting suicide. Our coworker wanted to go visit his friend to express his Christian love, encouragement, and concern, but he wasn't sure exactly what to say. He was worried about saying the wrong thing. He asked our group if we had any words of wisdom. Various people offered helpful thoughts: "You could say this . . . You could say that . . ."

Then our principal, a very wise Christian man, said, "You will have said everything you need to say just by walking through the door." In other words, show up. That's the most important thing you can do. The person in pain probably won't remember much, if anything, that you say, but he or she will remember that you showed up. That will be the greatest comfort.

> The person in pain probably won't remember much, if anything, that you say, but he or she will remember that you showed up.

This chapter is again for Group Two: loved ones, friends, and pastors of cancer sufferers. We can learn many lessons from the book of Job about how to offer comfort and not comfort, mostly the latter. That is because the majority of the book is the conversation between Job and his friends, and for the most part, the friends were not very comforting.

But the friends did one thing right: They showed up. We are introduced to them in Job 2:11-13. After Job has suffered the loss of his children, possessions, and health, we read:

> When Job's three friends, Eliphaz the Temanite, Bildad the Shuhite and Zophar the Naamathite, heard about all the troubles that had come upon him, they set out from their homes and met together by agreement to go

and sympathize with him and comfort him. When they saw him from a distance, they could hardly recognize him; they began to weep aloud, and they tore their robes and sprinkled dust on their heads. Then they sat on the ground with him for seven days and seven nights. No one said a word to him, because they saw how great his suffering was.

"Then they sat on the ground with him for seven days and seven nights." I think we have to commend Job's friends for that. They heard of their friend's pain. They wanted to sympathize with him and comfort him. So they showed up at his side. That is the most important thing you can do to comfort a cancer patient or anyone who is suffering. Show up.

As with so many things in the book of Job, the friends' silence is viewed in different ways. Some say their silence was cold and harsh—a sign of their lack of empathy. I disagree. I think their silent vigil with Job was the best thing they did. Sitting in silence with Job was at least a small measure of comfort.

So what do I say? What should I do?

Learn the positive lesson from Job's friends. They showed up. Countless fellow Christians showed up for Lisa and me. What follows are some of the examples. It's a long list and just scratches the surface.

Friends took Lisa to appointments when I was unable to do so. Some gave up most of their day to sit with her during her chemotherapy treatments.

For four months, friends brought us supper every other day so we would not have to worry about meal preparation. One day we would eat the delicious meal, and the next we would enjoy the leftovers. One of our wonderful friends organized this effort, and others selflessly gave of their time and love to feed us. Another friend routinely brought Lisa her favorite yogurt so she could indulge this pleasant craving.

Our daughter, a theater major, and five of her friends staged a play that raised some much appreciated funds to help with the bills. Countless people contributed to this production and the accompanying bake sale, which involved a lot of work.

Every chemo day, our daughter-in-law texted pictures of our grandchildren to Lisa.

The children for whom Lisa nannied made cards for her, played music with her, and most important, prayed with her and for her.

A wonderful woman from our church sent Lisa a card every week. Sometimes the card was cute, other times funny or sarcastic. It always added a little humor to the day. No matter what the card actually said, what it communicated was "I'm thinking of you."

I am the soccer coach at my school. A former player's mom, who had also gone through breast cancer, brought Lisa a blanket that she had sewn, which Lisa used to keep warm on chemotherapy days. Another friend, a talented seamstress, sewed beautiful headscarves for Lisa to wear during those months of chemo.

The family of our daughter's friend volunteered to host a joint graduation party so we would not have to worry about it. This saved us an enormous amount of time and concern.

Some friends planted a garden in our front yard, which we named our Friendship Garden, and filled it with beautiful plants and flowers. Lisa could look at it from our dining room window and think of the love of the people God has put in our lives.

Other friends walked with Lisa to make sure that she continued to exercise, which she needed to do but often needed encouragement to get started.

A woman from our church, who had gone through breast cancer a few years before my wife, found out when Lisa's first chemotherapy treatment was going to be. Unannounced, she went to the cancer center and arrived before my wife, just so that when Lisa walked through the door, she could see a friendly face and receive a hug and encouragement from this woman. The woman did this because she remembered how terrifying that first chemo treatment could be.

The list goes on and on.

All the cancer survivors I have spoken with brought this up again and again. The expressions of love and support they received from fellow Christians far outweighed the few Zophar-like, comfortless comments they heard. And the Christian love they received from others was perhaps the greatest and most obvious fulfillment of Romans 8:28—God working for good even in the midst of pain.

So learn from Eliphaz, Bildad, and Zophar. What was the best thing they did? They showed up. What's the best thing you can do for friends, loved ones, or fellow church members who have cancer? Show up.

Sit with them. Commiserate with them. You may feel the need to say something wise and spiritual, but sometimes it's best just to sit with them, ask them how they are, and listen. Look them in the eyes.

> Sit with them. Commiserate with them.

Let them know what you can do for them. Let them know you are praying for them. Communicate your love with deeds of Christlike love.

Chapter 13
COMFORT FROM THE HIDDEN GOD

If we believe in the God of the Bible and not in some other god of our own making, then we must accept that the God of the Bible is a hidden God. This, I believe, is one of the main messages of the book of Job.

When we believe the words of Isaiah 45:15, "Truly you are a God who has been hiding himself, the God and Savior of Israel," that means we do the following, just as God wanted Job to do. He doesn't tell us everything we want to know. He hides our future years here on earth from us. We don't know how long we will have here or what we will experience while we remain. But we do know the great and glorious future we will have because of our Savior, Jesus. God has not kept that a secret from us.

"You're asking a question."

"You're asking a question." Remember that these were among the first words of this book. I had questions for my doctor, but he wasn't going to answer them. I needed to learn that I couldn't really ask questions in that situation. If my doctor was a little impatient and perhaps a bit arrogant, he could have said, "You don't know anything. Don't ask questions. It's not time for questions."

When we truly believe that God is a hidden God, who in his wisdom has decided not to reveal everything about himself to us, that means we relinquish the right we think we have to demand explanations from him. "Why is this happening?" God doesn't have to explain. We simply are not allowed to know why everything happens. It's not time for questions. And that's okay. We don't need to know. We just need to trust the hidden God. He is almighty and loving. But we ask our questions anyway.

> We just need to trust the hidden God. He is almighty and loving. But we ask our questions anyway.

"Are you punishing me?"

"God, are you punishing me? Why are you punishing me? What did I do?" One clear message of Job is that suffering is never a punishment for sin. Job's friends never understood that and kept prodding at Job to confess the sins that caused his trouble. God's answer is that Jesus already suffered the punishment for our sins on the cross. He does not punish our sins twice.

To be sure, sometimes we suffer the consequences of our ill-advised or sinful actions. A man who constantly drinks to excess might suffer painful health issues later in life because of his drinking. A woman who can't control her anger and constantly lashes out at her family members may find herself estranged from them later on. Even with cancer, there are similar examples. If a doctor tells a man year after year to quit smoking and then the man develops lung cancer, there probably is a connection between his actions and subsequent cancer.

But I would contend that such instances are rare. We have to remember that many who continue to live outside the boundary of God's law do not suffer. Instead, they seem to prosper. Consider reading Psalm 73.

It is a pointless exercise to try and make some connection between our personal sin and our suffering. If you have cancer, do not waste any time or heartache trying to establish some connection between your suffering or life's patterns and God's punishment: "Did I eat too much of this? Did I engage in too much of that activity? That must be why I now have cancer. Did I sin against God too much when I was young, and this is his way of getting back at me?" Job and his friends spent 35 chapters trying to establish such a connection that simply did not exist. Learn from them and do not go down that dead-end road.

Cling to what God *has* revealed

When we believe that God is a hidden God, it doesn't mean that God is completely hidden. It just means we don't need to try to figure out and understand things God hasn't revealed. Let the hidden God remain hidden. We might speculate, but in our lifetimes we will never know what he has hidden from us. Remember that he still has revealed much about himself. Find your comfort in the things he has revealed.

What has God revealed? He has revealed that he is a God of love. The Bible is filled with passages that say this. Twice in 1 John chapter 4 is the simple phrase "God is love"

He has revealed that he is a God of love.

(verses 8,16). We could spend days reading all the passages that tell us God loves us. One of my favorites is Jeremiah 31:3: "I have loved you with an everlasting love." God has always loved you and always will. In Job's suffering, he eventually questioned the love of God. He saw God as mean, vindictive, and unjust. When Job thought this, he was wrong. As Elihu reminded him, "[God] does not oppress" (Job 37:23). Don't ever forget that! God loves you. He loves you so much that he died for you. As a shepherd cradles a lamb in his arms, so your loving Good Shepherd has you in his arms. Take refuge in that love even if you do not understand why you have been suffering trials.

What has God revealed? He has revealed that he wants you to be saved and with him in heaven: "God our Savior, who wants all people to be saved and come to a knowledge of the truth" (1 Timothy 2:3,4). That's why he sent Jesus to suffer and die for you. Cling to that Savior even in the darkest days of cancer.

God is a hidden God, but he is not completely hidden. He has revealed to us his beautiful, comforting promises. When we believe that God is hidden, we abandon the need to know everything about him and the answers to all our questions. Rather, we look to the promises God has revealed to us and cling to

> God is a hidden God, but he is not completely hidden.

them. In the throes of Job's terrible suffering, we often see him doing just that—he clung to the promises of God. Perhaps there is no greater expression of that faith than in Job 13:15: "Though he slay me, yet will I hope in him." Job's confession is simple: "Maybe all this pain is from God. Maybe it's from the devil. I don't know—but I will put my hope in my God." We learn from Job and say, "Oh, that we might have such a faith in the hidden God in the midst of pain!"

Romans 8:28: "We know that in all things God works for the good of those who love him."

A few chapters ago, I shared the observation that a suffering Christian can be Romans 8:28'd to death. If we hear that beautiful passage—or any passage of the Bible—over and over again, we can become numb to it or feel that others are saying these words without real sympathy or love behind them. Romans 8:28, as beautiful a promise as it is, can start to sound like the pious platitudes of Job's friends.

But the fact remains that Romans 8:28 is true. God works for good in all things, even evil and painful things like cancer. Believing that God is a hidden God means clinging to his revealed promises—promises like Romans 8:28.

God was working for good in Job's life

God was working for good even in the unimaginable suffering of Job. How? Perhaps it was to have Job's story recorded in the

Bible. His story teaches every generation of believers to learn the difficult lesson that God is a hidden God. Another benefit was that Job's friends were led to learn more about God and that they needed to beware of saying more about God than what had been revealed. For them, another reason was to confront their wrong attitudes with Job's confession and faith. Still another reason was that as Job humbled himself before God after God spoke to him, he was led to rely on God all the more in his life. But there were other lessons beyond what we might think.

God is working for good even in the lives of cancer patients

When we believe that God is a hidden God, we cling to what he has revealed, such as the promise that he is working for good in all things, even in the lives of cancer patients and their families.

What might be the good that God brings into your life, even through cancer?

I do not want to be like Eliphaz, Bildad, and Zophar and claim that I know for certain how God will work in your life when cancer comes to you or a loved one. But based on our experiences and the experiences of others, I offer some possibilities. Here they are.

The opportunities that others are given for Christian love

I shared several examples in the last chapter of the love Lisa and I were shown while she was going through treatment. There were many, many more. We were simply overwhelmed by the countless examples of Christlike love we experienced from our own family members, our extended family, and the fellow, everyday Christians in our area. We were blessed by people from all the congregations that support the school at which I am privileged to teach. We received love and support from people all over the country. It is impossible to recount all the examples of Christian love. We will always be thankful to these people. We will always be grateful to God for them.

> **Remember the positive lesson from Job's friends: Show up.**

Remember the positive lesson from Job's friends: Show up. That may be a way God is working for good in the life of a cancer patient and the lives of those who show up. He is using these people to be his loving hands in that patient's life. If you are suffering through cancer now, perhaps in the future you will be the instrument of God's grace in the life of someone else who will suffer what you have gone through.

Here are some other examples of friends showing up for others. A young woman who went through cancer treatment shared how lonely she would get and how precious it was to receive notes and visits from her friends. One friend would regularly come and just do simple household chores—things that the woman had difficulty summoning the energy to do. It was a simple gesture. It didn't require a lot of words of wisdom. But it was priceless encouragement to a person who was suffering.

Another friend went through intense chemotherapy on two separate occasions only a year apart. One of his friends, a high school teacher, would occasionally sneak away from school during his free hour just to sit with his cancer-stricken friend in the hospital room for a few minutes, sometimes not saying anything. This silent vigil meant the world to the sick friend. It was another example of God fulfilling his promise in Romans 8:28. God was working for good through the love of one of his children.

Remember what I told you about Mike and Jennifer. Mike learned that he had cancer at almost the same time Lisa learned about her cancer. As a result of Lisa's surgery, her cancer was removed from her body. Her treatment, by God's grace, helped extend her earthly life. It didn't turn out that way for Mike. When his cancer was discovered, it had advanced too far. Despite painful treatments, despite various drugs, Mike's earthly life was taken from him in a few short months. Jennifer was left without her husband, and their son, Chris, was left without his father. They were left with a lot of unanswered questions.

How was God working for good through Mike's experience? Well, I can tell you that whenever Lisa and I would see Mike at church, Bible class, or somewhere else, he was incredibly uplifting to us. Although he was in pain and his life was draining away, he hardly ever wanted to talk about himself. He always wanted to talk to Lisa about herself. He empathized with her in a way that few others could at the time. He was incredibly encouraging during those dark days for us, even though he was going through even darker days himself.

As a result of Mike's experience, we got to know Jennifer, who had gone through breast cancer when she was younger. She has become a wonderful friend and support to Lisa in her life.

And there were many others like that—people who were going through cancer treatment at the same time as Lisa or had gone through it previously. Being able to sit with others who truly understood what she was experiencing and commiserate with them was a God-given blessing. It was an example of God working for good even in something horrible like cancer.

Opportunities to share your faith

When Christians suffer and endure that suffering with patience, they are often given the opportunity to share their faith. Neighbors ask, "How are you doing?" Then the door opens for Christians to confess that things are very hard, but God is helping. The conversation might open the door wider to speak of God's promises of love and care. A friend of mine who had gone through cancer treatment worked in sales. I asked him how often he had the opportunity to talk about his faith as a result of his cancer. Without hesitation, his response was "Hundreds of times." People ask questions, such as "Where do you find your strength?" or "How do you face death?" These questions easily lead to conversations about God and what he has done for us—what he has revealed to us. They provide easy opportunities to tell people that yes, we will die, and cancer powerfully reminds us of that, but we know we will go to heaven after death. We confess that we will go there because we have a Savior who has taken away all our sins on the cross and rose from death to give us that hope and victory too.

We are powerfully reminded how much we need God

When we are in good health and life is going well, we don't always feel a great need for God in our lives. This was not the case for Job, of course. Even when his life was good, "he feared God and shunned evil" (Job 1:1). But Job's example isn't the case for most. When something like cancer lays us low and brings us to our knees, we are reminded that God is our only strength. As Paul learned after being afflicted with his thorn in the flesh, he could confess, "When I am weak, then I am strong." In Paul's suffering, God had reminded him, "My grace is sufficient for you, for my power is made perfect in weakness" (2 Corinthians 12:9,10). For the cancer sufferer drained of all physical strength, God's strength is all there is left to rely on. His strength will not disappoint. Lisa would be the first to tell you that she often felt bereft of her own strength during her cancer treatments. God is the one who saw her through it all.

Where is our true home?

> When we suffer, we are reminded that this life is not our eternal goal.

When we suffer, we are reminded that this life is not our eternal goal. Heaven is our goal. As Paul said in Romans 8:24, "Who hopes for what they already have?" If we had a perfect, pain-free life in this world, why would we look forward to heaven? We wouldn't. Paul went on, "If we hope for what we do not yet have, we wait for it patiently" (Romans 8:25). Painful experiences like cancer focus our attention on what we do not yet have—the pain-free, cancer-free, perfect life of bliss waiting for us in heaven. This is why Jesus came into this world—to suffer and die for us so that we might have heaven.

This also happened for Job. In the midst of his suffering, tormented in body and soul, beaten down by the accusations of his uncomforting friends, he still lifted his eyes to heaven and said, "I know that my redeemer lives, and that in the end he will stand on the earth. And after my skin has been destroyed, yet in my flesh I will see God; I myself will see him with my own eyes—I, and not another. How my heart yearns within me!" (Job 19:25-27).

Yes, God is a hidden God. Learn to accept that he and his plans are often hidden from us. Try not to become frustrated by questions he has not answered. Yet God is not completely hidden. He has revealed comfort upon comfort to us. Take refuge in that comfort. Go to his Word and promises again and again. That is where your heart will find peace.

CONCLUSION

This has been a book about a suffering man: Job. It has been written for people who are suffering from the terrible disease of cancer. As I finish this book, I would like to tell yet another story of suffering that includes some gruesome details. Please bear with me.

One of the greatest instances of mass human suffering in the history of the world was the Holocaust. Before and during World War II, the Nazis in Germany, under the leadership of Adolf Hitler, condemned millions of people, who were viewed as undesirable, to concentration camps. There the people were subjected to hard labor, torture, sickening medical experimentation, and starvation. Millions were ultimately sent to the gas chambers.

One prisoner at the concentration camp in Buna was a young boy, who was so kind and sweet that the other inmates considered him like an angel. One day, there was a theft at the concentration camp, and the authorities decided to make an example of three prisoners. One of the three was the young boy. The three victims were tortured and ultimately hanged. All the other inmates had to watch the brutal treatment and hanging. It was an especially horrifying moment in the midst of an unrelentingly horrifying experience.

It was bad enough that the young boy had to be tortured and then hanged. But because he was just a child and didn't weigh as much as the other victims, his death took longer. He struggled at the end of the noose for about 30 minutes, slow and agonizing, before he finally died. And all the other prisoners had to watch. Throughout this dreadful scene, one of the inmates in the crowd periodically asked, "Where is God? . . . Where is he? . . . Where is God now?"

Where is God? That became Job's question. In the midst of his pain he lamented, "If only I knew where to find him; if only I could go to his dwelling!" (Job 23:3). Maybe that has been your question also.

The story of the angel in the concentration camp was told in the book *Night* by Holocaust survivor Elie Wiesel. As a teenager incarcerated at Buna, Wiesel witnessed that stomach-churning scene and heard the anguished questions "Where is God? . . . Where is he? . . . Where is God now?" Wiesel had no answer to those questions. He wrote that, for him, God died that day.

I read about that story in a book written by Philip Yancey. Yancey is a well-known Christian writer, and his book is entitled *Where Is God When It Hurts?* As the title indicates, the book tackles the thorny question of suffering—how can God allow it? Yancey spent time with lepers and leprosy doctors. He interviewed many, believers and nonbelievers, who had suffered intensely. Of course, he analyzed the message of Job and how it applies to suffering.

Toward the end of Yancey's book, he told the story of Elie Wiesel and the horrifying sight of the angel's suffering and death at Buna. Yancey wrote that after immersing himself so much in the world of pain and pondering realities like that of Elie Wiesel and the Holocaust, he too was tempted to abandon his faith in the loving God of the Bible. He was also plagued by the same question that plagued Job: Where is God when it hurts—when people really, really suffer? Yancey was tempted to become a skeptic like Martin Sixsmith or an unbeliever like Elie Wiesel. In terrible times it is easy to ask, "Who can believe in a God who allows such pain in this world?"

But as often as Yancey thought about these examples of terrible suffering, he kept coming back to the cross of Christ. He wrote,

"God did not exempt even himself from human suffering. He too hung on a gallows, at Calvary, and that alone keeps me believing in a God of love" (Philip Yancey, *Where Is God When It Hurts?*, Grand Rapids: Zondervan, 1977, p. 160).

Job suffered. Crushed in body and spirit, he wondered where God was. He wanted answers that he never got. Why did he remain a believer? What sustained him? He was sustained by the same truth to which Philip Yancey kept coming back.

> Where is God? Answer: He is here with us. He is in our world.

Where is God? Answer: He is here with us. He is in our world. He did not stay in heaven, but he came here. He did not exempt himself from human suffering. He went to the cross to suffer for the sins of the entire human race. Matthew 8:17 says, "He took up our infirmities and bore our diseases." He took our sin—our cancer—and suffered. He endured suffering far beyond what we can conceive. Greater even than Job's suffering. Far greater than Job's suffering. Why? Because he loves us beyond what we can imagine.

That's why Job could cling to God even in his darkest days: "Though he slay me, yet will I hope in him" (Job 13:15). Sometimes Job thought that God was afflicting him. Sometimes he was bitter against God.

> "Though he slay me, yet will I hope in him."

But ultimately he knew that God was his Savior and that he could put his hope in this Savior-God. That's why he also could confess, "I know that my redeemer lives, and that in the end he will stand on the earth. And after my skin has been destroyed, yet in my flesh I will see God" (Job 19:25,26). Then Job will not ask, "Where is God?" Because he will be with God and see him with his own eyes.

That same faith sustained Lisa through her ordeal with cancer, through the answered and unanswered questions. This ordeal isn't over and won't be for the rest of Lisa's earthly life. That same faith continues to sustain her.

Why did God allow cancer into your life? What exactly does the future hold for you? Those answers are not for you to know because God is a hidden God. But you do know that God loves you. He suffered for you. He paid for all your sins on the cross. He is your Redeemer. You can put your hope in him.

With Job, you can say, "I know that my redeemer lives, and that in the end he will stand on the earth. And after my skin has been destroyed [maybe by cancer], yet in my flesh I will see God; I myself will see him with my own eyes" (Job 19:25-27).

With Paul, you can say, "I am convinced that neither death nor life, neither angels nor demons, neither the present nor the future, nor any powers, neither height nor depth, nor anything else in all creation [even cancer!], will be able to separate us from the love of God that is in Christ Jesus our Lord" (Romans 8:38,39).

You can be convinced of it because that is what the hidden God has revealed to you. That's what he wants you to know and believe.

POSTSCRIPT

Every few months, cancer patients go in for scans. If the patients have been cancer-free, the scans show if the cancer has returned. If the patients have cancer, the scans show if the cancer has spread, stayed the same, or gone into remission (hallelujah!). The hours or days the patient waits for the results are sometimes known as the time of "scanxiety."

In late December 2018, after four years of clean scans, Lisa's scan and subsequent biopsy revealed that her cancer had metastasized in her lower abdomen. There were a lot of tears in the Haag household that day because we now knew that Lisa would deal with cancer the rest of her earthly life.

For the next two years, her oncologists repeatedly told us that her cancer was "non-life-threatening" because it had not spread to any vital organs. So throughout 2019 and 2020, Lisa was treated with various medications, which often had nasty side effects. But for the most part she was able to live life relatively normally.

In 2021, Lisa began to experience more and more pain and started having trouble swallowing. In late March, she went into the hospital. A spinal tap revealed cancer cells in the fluid around her brain and spinal column. For the first time, we were informed that she did not have long to live. We thought probably a matter of months or weeks. It turned out to be only ten days. Lisa went to heaven on April 10, 2021, the Saturday after Easter.

During those last ten days, we spoke often about her imminent departure from this world and entrance into heaven. I think I cried many more tears than Lisa because I loved her so much and knew that I would miss her terribly. But she would comfort me. Isn't that the opposite of how it should be? The pastor-husband should comfort his suffering and dying wife. But Lisa would comfort me with her quiet, peaceful faith. She comforted me by reminding me that she was going to heaven to be with her resurrected Savior. Lisa was always a believer, and her faith in her Savior shone brightest in those last days.

Along with all widows and widowers, I now have the sadness of losing my beloved spouse. But I also have a great thankfulness to God for giving me such a wonderful Christian wife, keeping her in her faith, and now taking her out of this world of cancer and pain to her home in heaven. I look forward to when I will join her and all the saints around our Savior's throne.

The same faith in God's promises that sustained Job in the midst of his suffering sustained my wife, Lisa. I pray that you will find this same comfort and strength.